27
SPIRITUAL
GIFTS

Robert J. Hillman

Melbourne

27 SPIRITUAL GIFTS

National Library of Australia
  Cataloguing-in-Publication entry.

Hillman, Robert J.
  27 spiritual gifts.

  ISBN 0 85819 601 8.

  1. Gifts, Spiritual. I. Joint Board of Christian Education. II. Title.
  III. Title: Twenty-seven spiritual gifts.

234'.13

First printed 1986

Design: Robina Norton
Typeset: Bookset Pty Ltd
Printer: Globe Press Pty Ltd
JB86/1126

Published by The Joint Board of Christian Education
Second Floor, 10 Queen Street, Melbourne 3000, Australia

Foreword

All members of the people of God are indwelt and gifted by the Holy Spirit for life and ministry within the family, the church and the world. This mutual ministry of the whole body of Christ will be facilitated by applying insights from this book.

Here is a readable book for all and a useful tool for local church leaders. Drawing on a wide knowledge and understanding of spiritual gifts, it gives practical guidance on how to discover one's own gift, discern and affirm gifts in others and help develop and use them to the glory of our Lord Jesus Christ.

This book combines sound biblical and theological insights and practical experience in a parish situation, all refined over a number of years of teaching and consulting related to the New Testament teaching on spiritual gifts and its practical application.

Robert Hillman is highly regarded throughout the church in Australia as an authority in this field and is in great demand as a lecturer in the area of spiritual gifts. He brings a personal and intellectual integrity to his teaching and writing.

I warmly commend this book as a much-needed resource which I believe will encourage all aspects of ministry and enable quality and quantity growth in the Christian church.

John Mallison
Sydney
July 1986

Contents

Acknowledgments

I acknowledge my indebtedness to Professor C. Peter Wagner, of Fuller Seminary for first introducing me to a comprehensive treatment of spiritual gifts and to C. Mel Robeck Jnr of the same seminary for reading the first draft of this book. My thanks also go to Wendy Cowling for reading a later draft and to Carol Flack, Chris Wright, Pat Marshall, Elaine Sharoff and others for assisting in various ways with typing. My thanks to my secretary Kaye Johnson for her tireless efforts in putting the manuscript on computer. My thanks, too, to my wife Jeanette for assistance with correcting the manuscript and to the Joint Board of Christian Education for their patience in what has been a long project.

I especially acknowledge the contribution of countless people throughout the Australian church in many seminars over some eight years. I have read widely in commentaries, books and other articles and have sought to acknowledge in footnotes authors whose material has been quoted or relied on. There are no doubt many who have contributed in some way to my thinking who are not mentioned here.

DEDICATED
TO
ROZ, JEN and CHRIS

1

The church:
bus or body?

Until recent years the church in Australia reminded me of a bus
— a one person bus. (To be sure that was a distinct improve-
ment on a one *man* bus). The bus was operated by the one
person. He or she started the bus, collected the fares, stopped
the bus, provided the commentary, helped the people on and
off, effected running repairs, and negotiated with the bus company hierarchy. The operator was even expected to canvass for
new passengers, although to be honest there was seldom time
for this with so many other responsibilities. In fact most drivers
secretly believed that the fewer joining the bus the better — 'for
then they and the driver are better looked after'. Everything
happened 'up front'. The passengers sat in their parallel 'pews'
quite oblivious to one another. They were content to be 'trans-
ported'. As the hymn puts it: 'Oh what transport all divine'.[1]

At twelve midday, sharp, the bus stopped and let the passengers off. The operator was busy during the whole week keeping
that old bus going. He or she returned the next week to the
same place and at the same time to pick up the same passengers,
weather permitting!

In recent years things have improved. The bus has been up-
dated. It is no longer a one person bus. There are *many* 'conductors'. These conductors all dress in uniforms. They all look and
act alike. They all assist the operator. Indeed many operators
appear to be hanging on to the wheel like grim death. They fear
a take-over. Now almost everything, and sometimes more than
everything, is done by the conductors. To be sure, when every-

thing is running smoothly there is good co-operation between the operator and conductors. The conductors work on the principle of 'equal share of the work'. Each one looks after ten passengers — collects their fares, opens the windows, wakes them up at the right stop, and so on. And the passengers? They are dying off rapidly. Many are having heart attacks. There is simply nothing for them to do. (Previously they did open a window now and again). Some of the conductors are handing in their badges. They are simply no good at collecting fares and fulfilling many of their responsibilities. Besides, they think that the passengers will be better off without them.

Who are these conductors? All of them have a badge on their lapel with the letter 'L' on it. Some think that L stands for 'learner' (something like disciple). But one wonders whether these conductors will ever learn! Others think that L stands for 'leader'. But we know that this is no way to lead.

L must stand for 'L-der'. But Elder starts with 'E'. How can you expect them to do their job correctly? They can't even spell!

Let the elders not despair, however. Teaching on spiritual gifts may assist them to 'spell' out their job description in helpful, flexible and meaningful ways.

In the Bible the church is not like a bus. It is like a body. Christ is the head and every member a different but important part (1 Corinthians 12:12-31). There is nothing like a passenger in this body , not even an appendix. Every part has its own vital function and most parts have a different function.

The Bible teaches that every member of the church — of Christ's body — has a function. This means that everyone has a ministry. It also means that there is great variety in this ministry. If you are a hand you are not intended to be a foot. You must find your ministry and exercise that. If you are a Christian you are a member of a body — not a passenger on a bus.

The Uniting Church feels called to many ministries. The world cries out for food, justice, equality, peace, employment and authentic religion. Great also is the need of the church. Enormous effort and resources are called for if we are to serve the church and world of our day.

Many of our ordained and lay workers succumb to the heavy burdens of service. How can we adequately meet the complex demands of today without succumbing to the pressures of ministry?

A proper understanding of spiritual gifts can help us to get our priorities right and can provide vast human resources for ministry which the church has often overlooked. This can be done without any threat to the roles of the Ministers of the Word or elders. Their functions emerge more clearly defined and crucial, while at the same time considerable burdens are lifted from their shoulders.

1 Rev Wade Robinson, *Alexander's Hymns No 3*, Marshall, Morgan and Scott, No 193.

2

The church:
players or spectators?

In the first chapter we compared the church with a bus and with a body. The Australian church may also be compared with a football match. Towards the end of a tough grand final a small group of players stagger around the field desperately in need of rest. Around the oval is a huge crowd of adrenalin charged onlookers desperately in need of exercise.

In the church of Christ there can be no spectators. Everyone is a player. Each one has a ministry. Not everyone plays fullback. Everyone has his or her own position.

Ephesians chapter 4 supports this model of the church. The saints (i.e. all Christians) carry out the work of ministry (verse 12). All God's people are in the team. Everyone is a player. The leaders (verse 11) may be compared to player-coaches who assist all the other players to play in their correct positions and to play to the best of their ability.

Busy leaders and loyal members of the Australian church frequently complain about all they have to do and about the many onlookers in the church who seem content to cheer them on, or more likely, to disparage them from the sidelines. In this situation we often find individual players endeavouring to fill several positions at once, seldom freed to concentrate on playing in the position for which they are best gifted.

One of the things about exercising your special gifts is that service becomes a delight rather than sheer duty or drudgery. It remains a burden (Jesus used the term 'yoke') but it is a light burden (Matthew 11:28). It is accompanied by fruitfulness and fulfilment. Vigorous training throughout the week seems worthwhile when you are able to play effectively in your right position on Saturday afternoon.

A speaker was addressing a group of ordinands. He argued that those being ordained to the ministry were very fortunate indeed. They were like the mother of Moses who was commissioned by the Egyptian princess to look after her own son. She was doing what she delighted to do and yet was being paid for it!

Unlike the mother of Moses, or the professional footballer, you may not get paid for exercising your gift but it will bring you great delight as you serve God your Saviour in a ministry for which he has equipped you. Normally, you will be able to cope. You will feel yourself to be effective, accomplishing goals and doing the job well. You will have a certain efficiency. Others will affirm you in your particular ministry. You will not feel like a square peg in a round hole, or like a winger playing fullback. You will have to train hard: there will be sweat and frustration (Romans 8:22, 23, 36) but generally your ministry will be fruitful. You will feel (as you receive sufficient training), 'This is what I do best — for God and for others'.

The ministry may be quite confined and unspectacular. (It may not be in the forward line!) It may not seem very 'spiritual'. But it will be strategic both in itself and because it frees other Christians to concentrate on their gifts.

You will find as you play in your natural position in the team concentrating on your spiritual gift, that your efficiency increases dramatically. You will generally accomplish much more in the time available than if you are involved in a ministry for which you have no special gift. Generally, this ministry will involve much less stress because you are not continuously frustrated by a sense of inadequacy. The player who runs all over the field wastes energy and hampers the other members of the team.

There *is* such a thing as misplaced team loyalty. A person who plays Sunday school teacher for years despite the fact that he or she has no real teaching gift is probably missing his or her God-given ministry. Of course there is need to try oneself out in various positions including teaching to see which is one's area of giftedness. There may be occasions, when for a short period, one should substitute as a teacher, because of the need. But generally a long-term ministry which does not involve the use of one's best gifts appears to be unbiblical. It is as tragic in terms of Christian service as is the ruining of one's football career by continuing to play fullback instead of forward.

In my book on quality church growth I emphasised the importance of mobilizing the whole congregation in response to the Great Commission[1]. If the church is to grow at its maximum rate everyone in the congregation needs to orientate his or her thinking and ministry around the fulfilment of the Great Commission. The mobilization of the laity is *the* key to church growth.

Here we need to sound a warning. There have been many attempts to mobilize the whole church for evangelism, but many of these have been dismal failures. This is mainly because of a failure to follow the biblical teaching on spiritual gifts. I well remember hearing about the church whose minister called the whole church to become involved in a program of visitation evangelism. One of the faithful members who had no special gift for evangelism had a heart attack at the first door. This venture failed because it was assumed that everyone could play in the one position.

In 1974 a team from the Fuller Evangelistic Association visited Rev. Wayne Pohl's St. Paul's Lutheran Church, Trenton Michigan, to conduct a church growth seminar. As a result a key decision was made — to help members discover and use their spiritual gifts. In contrast to the previous example, every member was assisted to find his or her correct position. The results were dramatic — Sunday morning attendance rose from 318 in 1975 to 896 in 1982. In the same period the budget increased from $118,000 to $603,000 while Sunday school attendance rose from 210 to over 800.[2]

This truth may be applied not only to the church (team) but also to the individual member (player). Melanie was a member of my confirmation class. She was divorced, very short and not very well educated. In the class were several other people who were very gifted and well-educated. In this group Melanie had trouble with her large-sized inferiority complex. She did not think that there was any special position in the team which was reserved for her.

It soon became obvious to all that Melanie could answer the questions when no one else could. She seemed to know more than all the others put together. It was obvious that she had a spiritual gift which enabled her to acquire readily a knowledge of God's Word and to share it with others.

Soon she was teaching Scripture in school. She began a course in theology which she has since completed. She conducts her own adult Bible study group each week. It was a beautiful thing to see Melanie blossom as she realised that *she* had a special gift from God. There was something in life which she could do — and do well.

In 1982 I contracted lymphoma — cancer of the lymph glands. My church released me from all administrative responsibilities so that I could concentrate on a teaching and pastoral ministry. Although my physical condition did not permit me to lead the parish team I was able, with a minimum of stress to accomplish a great deal in terms of writing, study, teaching and pastoral ministry. Now in a new type of ministry, I come to an undisturbed office and spend my time in prayer and writing. I frequently take teaching missions and minister to needy people in the parish and beyond (especially those who have terminal diseases). It is possible that I am accomplishing much more for the kingdom of God in this limited way than I was previously with a multitude of responsibilities. Why? Because I have been freed to concentrate on exercising my spiritual gift.

It is not simply a matter of each one finding his or her correct position in the team. Everyone must play the game with the right spirit. In Christian terms the 'right spirit' refers to the Holy Spirit which everyone who believes in Christ receives (Acts 2:38; Romans 8:9). The Holy Spirit who indwells each serving believer gives the church a spirit of unity (or team spirit) under Christ the head of the church (or captain of the team).

Many a player has spoiled his game or even been sent from the field (or to the sin-bin) because of a bitter spirit which has led to dirty play. Our inner lives (including our memories) will need to be clean if our spiritual gifts are to be effective. No doubt this is the greatest hindrance to the exercise of our gifts. It is probably the main reason for the ineffectiveness of much of the church's service and mission. We may call these inner weaknesses 'spirit barriers'. These barriers can lead to the loss of the game despite the fact that everyone is playing in their right position and that on paper the team appears unbeatable. We shall need to look at this point again.

The way ahead for us in the Australian church is to structure ways to help our ministers of the Word, elders and members find their gifts and exercise them in strategic and effective ways for the building up of the church and the winning of and serving the world. We must also assist all our people to serve in the power of the Spirit and to deal with inner attitudes which restrict the Spirit's working.

1 R. J. Hillman, *The Church: Growing Up and Growing Out*, Unichurch, 1981, p.25f.
2 C. Peter Wagner, 'Gifts and Growth: A Case Study' *Leadership* 111, 1, Christianity Today, 1982, pp.92-99.

3

General truths about spiritual gifts

Before we examine individual gifts in some detail let us consider some general biblical truths concerning gifts.

Gifts and grace

Paul uses several different Greek words to refer to gifts. His favourite word is *charisma* (gift; the plural is *charismata*). This word is closely related to a very important word in Pauline theology — charis which means 'grace'. Paul uses this word *charis* approximately one hundred times. It means God's unearned favour, or love, and sometimes power, which comes to us through the crucified Christ in abundant measure. By choosing charismata as his word for gifts Paul wishes to say that these gifts are never earned but are always freely given by the God of abundant grace.

Now the only proper response to grace is gratitude — never pride or envy. Sometimes churches or groups are divided by an unbiblical approach to gifts. Pride concerning gifts received may readily lead to division. This reveals a basic misunderstanding of spiritual gifts as grace-gifts which are given to build up the church and never divide it.

Gift and gifts

The gift (person) of the Holy Spirit is received when one becomes a Christian. Peter announced to earnest seekers on the day of Pentecost: 'Repent and be baptised every one of you in the name of Jesus Christ for the forgiveness of your sins; and you shall receive the gift of the Holy Spirit' (Acts 2:38).

The gifts of the Spirit on the other hand, are special abilities which the Spirit of God gives to assist Christians to serve Christ, one another and the world. We can say, then, that everyone who receives the gift (person) of the Spirit of God receives at least one of the gifts (special abilities).

Gifts and fruit

The fruit of the Spirit 'is love, joy, peace, patience, kindness, goodness, faithfulness, gentleness, self-control' (Galatians 5:22-3). This fruit, especially love, takes priority over the gifts (special abilities) of the Spirit (1 Corinthians 12:31-13:13). It is very important to observe from the beginning that without the fruit of the Spirit the gifts are of no value. It is only as the gifts are exercised with the fruit of the Spirit that they can reach their full potential and bring glory to God.

We note, too, that although all the fruit should be growing in every Christian not every gift is given to every Christian. Indeed the gifts are shared among the body (the church). Each Christian has differing gifts in order that each member of the body may complement every other member.

Gift barriers

The fruit of the Spirit and the gifts of the Spirit can only be released and come to fulness in the person who has 'a pure heart and a good conscience and sincere faith' (1 Timothy 1:5). Bitterness, resentment, fear, anxiety, impurity, covetousness, dishonesty, impatience and many other attitudes grieve the Spirit of God and hinder his working.

We all need to spend a good deal of time in the study of Scripture (with other Christians as well as in private) and in meditation so that God will expose and cleanse those inner areas of life which are barriers to the free working of the Spirit in his fruit and gifts.

In addition some Christians may need some special therapy such as the healing of memories or psychiatric counselling in order to release them from a debilitating past.

16

Gifts and talents

Spiritual gifts are not to be identified with natural talents. Natural talents are given at birth (or perhaps conception). Every human being is talented — although many talents are not developed or are left to waste away. Spiritual gifts are given as a result of new birth. Since it is the one God who is active in both birth and new birth there is a relationship (or correlation) between natural talents and spiritual gifts.

There is, however, also a contrast between the two. Due to the sovereignty of God's Spirit we cannot always predict what amazing gifts God will give to those who receive the Holy Spirit. The sovereign Spirit is able to take a very ordinary person who does not appear to be greatly talented and give that person a remarkable ability for ministry.

This means that we must be on our guard in selecting people for office in the church. It is not always the person who is highly endowed with natural talents who is Christ's chosen one for office but the one who has been given the appropriate gift (and who exhibits suitable graces) who is most suitable.

No Christian ought to think of him or herself in an inferior way. Not only is he or she loved infinitely by the loving Father. He or she is also a very gifted person. And the sovereign Spirit seems to delight in giving gifts to very ordinary persons and in using them in remarkable ways in service.

Body gifts

Spiritual gifts are not given primarily for the sake of the individual but for the sake of the body (the church). See 1 Corinthians 12:7,12. The grace that is given is serving grace. It is given in order to assist the members of the body to serve one another. Any gift (such as the gift of speaking in tongues in private) which does not build up the body, but only the individual, should not be valued as highly as those gifts which contribute to the strengthening of the fellowship of the church.

If any one gift is to have its maximum effect, then it must draw on the gifts of the remainder of the body. The person, for example, who has a gift of visionary faith or of prophecy must realize that his or her personal visions or prophecies need the insight and other benefits which come from other gifts. Again we see the complementary nature of the gifts which promotes the unity and interdependence of the church.

Complex of gifts

Although each Christian has at least one special gift many have a group or complex of gifts. Ephesians 4:11 suggests that one combination of gifts is that of pastor-teacher, i.e. the one person possesses both a pastoring and a teaching gift. Teaching-knowledge seems to be a common combination, especially in the scholar-teacher. Leadership-faith appears to be an important combination for the leader of a growing church or parish. Administration-evangelism was important in the ministry of John Wesley. Administration-teaching seems also to be a common combination.

There appears to be no end to the variety of combinations of gifts. Some for example are pastor-teachers while others are teacher-pastors. This means that the second gift assists the primary gift. Some very gifted Christians may have a primary complex of gifts supported by a secondary complex. For example a person with a knowledge-teaching-pastoring primary complex of gifts may well have a combination of celibacy-voluntary poverty-giving as a secondary complex. The point is that you and I have our own unique combination of gifts. As we discover what these gifts are, we learn important truths about ourselves and are thus able to take up the ministries which best suit the gifts God has decided to give us.

Special and general gifts

In what follows there is a list of twenty-seven special gifts, most of which are mentioned in Scripture. There may be others which are not listed in the New Testament or here in this book. In addition, I want to suggest that corresponding to most of the special gifts, none of which is given to all Christians, are general gifts, all of which are given to every Christian.

For example, while only some Christians are prophets (1 Corinthians 12:29), virtually every Christian may prophesy (Acts 2:17-18). In the early church there were groups of prophets who prophesied regularly (because they had a special gift of prophecy) although any Christian could prophesy from time to time as the Spirit of God moved him or her to do so. I assume that this is the case with most of the spiritual gifts. Although some Christians have a special gift of evangelism (i.e. a special ability in communicating the gospel to unbelievers), all Christians have a general ability in this area.

We may say then that all Christians should be G.P's (exercising their general gifts in every area of service). They should also be specialists, wherever possible concentrating on their special gifts (rather than involving themselves in ministries which use only their general gifts).

Gifts are ministers and abilities

For more than one reason it appears quite incorrect and arbitrary to distinguish the type of gifts in Ephesians from those in 1 Corinthians and Romans. Some gifts, for example, are common to all three passages. All the gifts listed in 1 Corinthians 12:8-10 are abilities. In verses 28-30 ministers and abilities are mixed, although in the Revised Standard Version they all read like ministers. The original text says that God placed the following in the church:

ministers	abilities
apostles	powers
prophets	gifts of cures
teachers	helps
	governings
	various tongues

In Romans 12:6-8 Paul does the reverse. He begins by speaking about abilities and proceeds to speak about ministers:

abilities	ministers
prophecy	the one teaching
service	the one exhorting
	the one sharing
	the one taking the lead

In Ephesians 4:11 the gifts are ministers. They are not, as some affirm, non-personal ministries. They are people — apostles, prophets, evangelists, pastors and teachers.

It appears that in the key passages on spiritual gifts there is no sharp distinction between gifts as abilities and gifts as ministers. The emphasis in these passages seems to be on what the people *do* (a function) rather than on the office they hold. It is probably correct to assume that each minister (for example teacher) will have a corresponding ability (for example teaching). In any case it seems wisest for us in setting out our list of gifts to follow the New Testament pattern and include some which are special ministers and some which are special abilities.

19

4

Speaking gifts

Introduction

There are many different ways of grouping spiritual gifts. I prefer a simple approach suggested by 1 Peter 4:10,11 and divide them into speaking and serving gifts.

I have begun with the speaking gifts because some of them receive primary emphasis in Scripture (for example Ephesians 4:11; 1 Corinthians 12:28). I begin with the list of gifts in Ephesians 4 because I consider that in the New Testament they are the primary gifts. As Markus Barth points out, all of the Ephesians gifts are speaking gifts. This is because the church lives by the proclamation of the Word. Without that proclamation there is no mission and no Christian service.[1]

It should be noted however that there is no priority implied beyond the first five gifts (apostle, prophet, evangelist, pastor and teacher). The service gifts could easily have been included after 'teacher'. They are of enormous importance not only in authenticating the message proclaimed through the speaking gifts but also in being channels of God's love to all.

It is only as a matter of convenience, then, that I have listed and described all the speaking gifts before proceeding to treat the service gifts. In practice they can never be separated. There is a certain priority as far as the first few speaking gifts are concerned. (This reflects the priority in the church of proclaiming the gospel). The two types of gifts operating together however, are indispensable for the church's life and witness.

Gift 1
Apostle
Ephesians 4:11

For several years I have conducted spiritual gifts seminars. I had drawn up a list of twenty-seven New Testament gifts. These were arranged without any attention to priority. Since the gift of apostle was so complex and apparently of little general relevance and interest to today's church I gave it no priority in the list and hoped that no one would ask me a question about it! However, I began to study this gift in greater detail and I realised that it was basic for the life of the whole church and for a proper presentation of the New Testament teaching on gifts. I have re-arranged my list of gifts with 'apostle' at the top.

The church is founded upon both the apostles (and may we say New Testament prophets). 'Apostle' appears first in Ephesians 2:20 and in all Paul's lists of gifts (1 Corinthians 12:28,29; Ephesians 4:11). Christ himself is the chief corner stone. The apostles bear witness to him. They are his ambassadors. Their importance lies in that witness. Once the church ceases to be apostolic it ceases to be Christian. If the apostles are not the foundation Jesus Christ is not the corner stone.

All other gifts fall to the ground once the church loses its apostolic foundation. When the church moves away from the apostolic message — the teaching of the apostles — it ceases to be charismatic. All the gifts are dependent on that one gift. The church ceases to be Christian and charismatic (gifted) when it ceases to be apostolic. Remove the proclaimed message (kerygma) of the apostles — their witness to the risen Christ — and the church collapses. The central message (kerygma) and the teaching (didache) of the apostles as set out in the New Testament are essential marks of the apostolic church.

As we shall see there is controversy concerning the continuance or otherwise of this gift. Was it confined to the apostolic age? There appear to be individuals in the life of the church who perform some of the functions of the original apostles. It seems best, however, to regard this gift today as residing essentially in the corporate church. Some individuals may be regarded as apostles in a secondary sense because they exhibit in a special measure the marks of apostleship. The fullness of this gift however, resided in the original apostles and now belongs to the whole church which is founded on their message and which shares their mission.

The gift of apostle today

There are several current views:

1 The apostolic ministry belonged to the apostolic age. When the foundation of the church was laid the task of the apostles was complete. John W. Stott argues that in the primary sense the apostles have no successors although there are, no doubt, apostles today in the secondary sense of missionaries.[2]

2 The apostolic ministry was discontinued due to the fact that the church was not ready for it. As a result other gifts ceased as well.

3 The apostolic ministry is necessary only on particular occasions. This was Calvin's view.

4 The apostolic ministry is a constant ministry in the church. Markus Barth thinks that Ephesians 4:7-12 would be meaningless if apostles and prophets were no longer present and active in the congregations.[3] Of those who support this fourth view there are several varying views as to the function of the contemporary apostle.

a General leadership
Professor C. Peter Wagner sees this as a special ability of general authoritative spiritual leadership over a number of churches.[4]

b Preserving purity of doctrine (Acts 2:42)
The Christian theologian is a good example of one who instructs others with the truth of the gospels as displayed in apostolic Scripture so that they will be able to pass it on to others.[5]

c Planting new churches
Bridge and Phypers recognise that the twelve and Paul were apostles in a special, unrepeatable sense. They also argue that the gift of apostleship can be seen most clearly today in b above and in the activities of those who have been used of God in the extension of the church into new areas for the past two thousand years.[6]

22

Many commentators do not confine the apostolic gift to those who plant new churches but see it essentially as the modern day missionary gift.

5 The gift may be exercised in part by individuals who fulfil apostolic functions in the church. We who have our roots in the Reformed and Wesleyan tradition might think of Calvin, Knox and Wesley as apostles of the faith. Or today we might think of chairpersons of presbyteries, certain theologians of the Spirit, or missionary statesmen and women as fulfilling apostolic functions.

6 Arnold Bittlinger argues that although the ministries for the whole church (apostle, prophet etc.) are as significant as ever, they are often exercised not by individuals but by groups of people fulfilling apostolic and prophetic tasks.[7]

Conclusion

It apears best in describing the whole church as basically apostolic to emphasise first, the reliability of the message which the church proclaims concerning the risen crucified Christ and second, the evangelistic and missionary nature of the church. The apostolic church has a reliable Christ-centred message. It also has a mission. It is a 'sent' church.

During Jesus' earthly life his close followers were learners (disciples). After the resurrection they were 'sent ones' (apostles). They, like the church itself, had a message and a mission.

Emil Brunner once said that the church exists by mission as a fire exists by burning. That is certainly true of the church in the Acts of the Apostles. The pattern for the church to follow in every age is established there! The *Basis of Union* of the Uniting Church in Australia, paragraph 2, affirms: 'The Uniting Church lives and works within the faith and unity of the One Holy Catholic and Apostolic Church'. Paragraph 3 begins 'The Uniting Church acknowledges that the faith and unity of the Holy Catholic and Apostolic Church are built upon the One Lord Jesus Christ. The Church preaches Christ the risen crucified one and confesses him as Lord to the glory of God the Father'. Paragraph 5 affirms: 'The Uniting Church acknowledges that the Church has received the books of the Old and New Testaments as unique prophetic and apostolic testimony, in which she hears the Word of God and by which her faith and obedience are nourished and regulated'.

Let the church *be* what it affirms — apostolic in teaching and lifestyle — in message and mission! It is founded on apostolic witness to the risen crucified Christ. Let the church (and each of its members) be apostolic so that it may be authentically charismatic, displaying the whole range of gifts for the glory of Christ its head, in true unity in Christ, and for the sake of its varied ministries in the church and world.

Gift 2
Prophet
Ephesians 4:11

June Stephenson had been appointed to the parish staff. She had had a glorious conversion and had been influential amongst the young people for many years. When she resigned from her engineering position to take up this full-time ministry the church was overjoyed.

Within a few months tension had arisen. June was determined to 'do her own thing' without consulting the minister and elders. Indeed she used her great popularity amongst the youth and membership of the church to undermine the authority of the minister and create division within the church. Lesley Brown, the minister, was very concerned and gave herself to much prayer over the matter.

As she studied the Scriptures daily two passages appeared to be particularly relevant to this situation. She took these passages to June Stephenson and challenged her gently but firmly. She shared her concern over the division in the parish and said, 'June I believe I have a prophetic word for this situation. This prophecy consists in two passages of Scripture which I believe speak directly to our parish at this time. Now I realise that every prophecy must be tested (1 Corinthians 14:29). I am therefore open to be corrected by you or by the elders. I wish to read these passages and ask for your response. They are 1 Corinthians 1:10-13 and Hebrews 13:17'.

There are two possible endings to this hypothetical anecdote. Perhaps June realised the error of her ways and became a catalyst for unity within the parish. Perhaps Lesley Brown had to invite the elders to support her. We can almost be certain that the word of prophecy was the Spirit's instrument for healing to the body of Christ in that situation.

Definition of prophecy

The gift of prophecy is the special ability and call which the sovereign Spirit gives to some members of the church to receive and proclaim inspired authoritative contemporary messages to the world, the church, or to individuals.

Prophecy is not just any kind of preaching. It is directly inspired. It brings a direct message from God. It may in addition emphasize the way of salvation as on the day of Pentecost (Acts 2:17, 38, 39; Ephesians 3:5f).

The New Testament prophet usually brought a specific word so that the Christian community and the individual believers might know God's will. Barnabas, Paul and Timothy were separated to their ministries by prophecy (Acts 13:1f; 1 Timothy 1:18; 4:14). The prophet by his direct messages from God spoke to Christians for 'their upbuilding and encouragement and consolation' (1 Corinthians 14:3; see especially Acts 15:32). Through his or her direct and powerful preaching the secrets of human hearts were disclosed (1 Corinthians 14:25).

Prophecy in Paul often included a revelation (1 Corinthians 14:6). It could bring about conviction of sin (1 Corinthians 14:24f) as well as comfort and encouragement (1 Corinthians 14:3). David Hill believes that one form of modern prophecy is a specific type of pastoral preaching which includes a strong element of exhortation. It is generally very down to earth and specific.[8]

In addition to the above we may say that the original New Testament prophets although *forth*tellers rather than *fore*-tellers were nevertheless concerned about the future. They were concerned to prophesy concerning the Coming Age (Revelation 22:6f). But they also prophesied concerning contemporary events (Acts 11:28; 21:10f).

Christian prophecy begins and ends with Jesus. He is its inspiration, example and message. He is the prophet. In a sense there is no other prophet. Prophecy has its fulfilment and end in him. Christian prophecy finds its reality in Christ. Apart from him it is an abstraction. It is false prophecy. The Christian, then, who has some gift of prophecy (and every Christian may from time to time exercise a general gift of prophecy) must find his or her inspiration and message in Jesus Christ. Those amongst us who have a special gift of prophecy need to give much time to prayer and the study of Scripture (especially the gospels) so that we will be inspired men and women who continuously live near to Jesus the Christ. The Uniting Church sees itself as a prophetic church. It seeks to be contemporary and relevant. While it seeks to be catholic (universal) it seeks also to be Australian. Many of its preachers see themselves as prophetic — speaking a contem-

26

porary word to our nation and our time. On issues like unity, hunger, poverty, racism and warfare our preachers thunder out their messages like the prophets of old.

Perhaps God has called the Uniting Church into being partly to fulfil a prophetic role. (Is it not possible that the sovereign Spirit gives liberal quantities of particular gifts to particular churches and denominations?) If prophecy is our gift and calling then we are called to great things for Paul gives top priority to prophecy.

The nations of our day appear to be intent on destroying themselves through secularism, militarism, materialism and injustice. Problems relating to the disintegration of marriage and the family, homosexuality, unemployment, justice for Aborigines and many other contemporary issues cry out for an authentic prophetic word from God.

If our church is to exercise its prophetic gift responsibly and bring a word from God on each of these issues it must remember the following.

The prophetic church is first of all an apostolic church. The church is founded on the apostles and prophets (Ephesians 2:20). The prophetic church which was inaugurated on the day of Pentecost with the pouring forth of the Spirit is an apostolic church. Its overseers were the apostles led by Peter. Its converts gave themselves to study of the apostles' teaching. For us, the apostles' teaching which is nicely summarised in the Apostles Creed, is written for us in considerable detail in the New Testament. Unless we are true to that apostolic teaching and apostolic mission, we shall never be a truly prophetic church. Our prophecy may well be false prophecy.

More important still — Christian prophecy is centred in Christ. It can never be abstracted (i.e. cut off) from him. Prophecy is nothing unless it is relevant. It brings a contemporary word to the church and the world. Its relevance consists in its witness to Christ. Humanism is not Christian prophecy. Moralism is not prophecy. Being a conscience to the modern world is not necessarily fulfilling our prophetic mandate. John Wesley often said: 'I offered them Christ'. To be sure, that Christ-word must be penetratingly contemporary or it is not prophetic. But the prophetic word must be a Christ-word.

Authentic prophecy is inspired by the Spirit. It is a spiritual gift. One cannot be a Christian prophet unless one is filled with the Spirit. Commenting on contemporary life can be a substitute for spirituality. And topical sermons can be a substitute for Spirit-empowered preaching. The flesh and the Spirit are in opposition to one another. There is, therefore, nothing less prophetic than topical preaching which is delivered in the power of the flesh.

But note that this gift which comes near the top of Paul's list brings together what we in the Uniting Church have always affirmed belong together:

Spirituality and relevance
Christ and contemporary culture
Inspiration and concrete demand
The church and the world

The prophetic word

There are those who claim that the gift of prophet was no longer required when the foundation of the church was laid (Ephesians 2:20) and when the witness of the apostles and prophets to the Christ had been recorded in New Testament Scripture.

It appears that the completion of the New Testament canon made the church more prophetic not less. It is also possible that the completion of the New Testament called forth the continuing gift of prophecy in order that the prophetic Scripture might be applied in ever relevant ways to concrete situations.

The scriptural word is perennially contemporary. It is prophetic in that:

It witnesses to the prophet of God and unveils the hidden mysteries as it reveals the Christ of God.

It tells forth the living Word of God. Both Old and New Testament prophets are primarily forthtellers who bring a living inspired word to the human predicament. This living scriptural word as the instrument of the living Spirit remains contemporary — devastatingly so — 'For the Word of God is living and active, sharper than any two-edged sword, piercing to the division of soul and spirit, of joints and marrow, and discerning the thoughts and intentions of the heart' (Hebrews 4:12).

It foretells the future. The New Testament witness to Christ is clearly presented within an eschatological context i.e. the whole view of reality is viewed in the light of the coming age.

So the scriptural prophetic word is (through the Spirit) always related to the present and the future. It is a concrete contemporary word for the present. It is a word that is full of hope concerning the future.

The true contemporary prophet prophesies out of an apostolic church, according to Scripture which is both apostolic and prophetic. This Word is the sword of the Spirit. The spiritual gift of prophecy may never by-pass the prophetic scriptural word of the Spirit. Thus every contemporary prophecy must be in accord with that Word and must be tested by that Word. False prophecy arises when there is a separation of prophecy from Scripture. Prophecy at its best will be the inspired application of specific truths of Scripture to the real world of our day. The true prophet is a channel of the prophetic Word. He or she permits the Word to be what it is — the living Word, always contemporary, always specific, always the Word of the Spirit bearing witness to the Christ of God.

Gift 3
Evangelist
Ephesians 4:11

This is not a true story — yet. Perhaps it will become so in your parish!

The growth of All Saints Church had plateaued. After considerable transfer growth Sunday morning attendances had levelled off at about 100. There was of course plenty to keep the minister and everyone else busy! The details of the daily church program filled a large notice sheet every Sunday morning. But John and Kathy were deeply concerned about the lack of conversion growth. They had recently had teaching on spiritual gifts and felt that they had evangelistic gifts. After earnest prayer they sought the blessing of the minister and elders to establish an Evangelistic Task Force consisting of those who sensed an evangelistic gift and of others with a deep concern for conversion growth.

Two years later this group has become a catalyst for amazing growth in the church. Morning congregations are seldom below 150 and newcomers are often new converts. The task force has arranged a seminar on spiritual gifts and another on evangelism. Also, the following resulted:

Evangelistic support groups of several pairs (most of whom sense an evangelistic gift) have been formed. They pray together and report back to the group after going out for 'friendship evangelism' or after having coffee evenings for neighbours (during which evenings the Christian faith is explained in simple terms).

In addition, a **Lay Witness Team** which witnesses within the local parish area and in other parishes has been formed. Series of home meetings are held in which members of the team share their Christ-centred testimonies with non-churchgoers who are invited to coffee.

A mini mission under a visiting evangelist has been held. Several professed conversion and are being followed up.

It is interesting to note that the gift of evangelist does not appear in the list given in 1 Corinthians 12:28, whereas in Ephesians 4:11 it appears before 'pastor-teacher'. Thus pastors and teachers are preceded by the evangelists who have a certain missionary function. The situation is much the same as it was in Matthew's Gospel where Jesus appears as the evangelist awakening faith. Only then does he emerge as the teacher. If this interpretation is correct it follows:

> The evangelist fulfils a certain apostolic function in calling people to faith — in preaching the gospel (1 Timothy 2:7; 2 Timothy 1:11). An apostolic church is one which emphasizes evangelism.

> Evangelism precedes teaching. Teaching can never dispense with evangelism. The Christian faith is firstly evangelistic. In an important sense the proclamation of the good news precedes the teaching of the Word.

Herein may lie the chief reason for the non-growth of many Australian churches (especially Uniting Churches). It is often assumed that all who attend only need to be taught rather than also be evangelised. In this situation, conversion growth seldom takes place. Worse still, where it is assumed that outsiders do not need to be evangelised — merely taught the Christian faith — then new disciples are not generally won.

The word evangelist (*euangelistes*) occurs only three times in the New Testament (Acts 21:8, Ephesians 4:11 and 2 Timothy 4:5) although the number of evangelists must have been greater than one might suppose from the number of occurrences in the New Testament (Philippians 4:3; 2 Corinthians 8:18; Colossians 1:7; 4:12). In each of the three passages where the word 'evangelist' occurs evangelists are distinguished from apostles. Originally, it seems that all the apostles were evangelists and with their passing this gift assumes greater importance.

Originally 'evangelist' probably referred to functions (what the evangelist did) rather than a specific office in the church. So today although a few will be appointed as evangelists most exercise their evangelistic function informally and unofficially. It may be, however, that denominations like the Uniting Church should give priority to the appointment of evangelists. If enormous efforts are rightly expended and large sums given in order to send missionaries to other cultures, should we not be prepared to spend similar amounts in the evangelism of our nation?

Not every Christian has a special evangelistic gift although every Christian has a general evangelistic — witness gift.

(Some church growth strategists like Peter Wagner have found that approximately ten percent of an average congregation appears to have this special gift.) This understanding of the gift of evangelism rescues the church from both a guilt and opting-out mentality in regard to evangelism.

Many Christians are plagued with guilt when they find themselves to be much less effective in evangelism than others (whom they do not realise have a special gift in this direction).

One of the great dangers of gift-theology, especially if it is presented without proper biblical balance is that it too easily absolves individual Christians from responsibility in those areas of ministry in which they have no special gift. I am presenting here a concept of charisma in which the whole church shares in all the gifts corporately, and to some extent, individually. Pentecost inaugurated the age of the Spirit when the Spirit was poured out on all so that all believers might prophesy (Acts 2:17). Could they not also exercise other gifts of the Spirit? When persecution arose against the Jerusalem church 'they were all scattered . . . except the apostles . . . Now those who were scattered went about preaching the word' (Acts 8:1-4). It is a remarkable thing that only those who had a special evangelistic gift (the apostles) stayed in Jerusalem! It was those who (presumably) mostly did not have this gift who 'went about preaching the word'.

It is extremely interesting to note, however, that Luke goes on to describe the effective ministry of Philip who is later described as an evangelist (Acts 8:5f; 21:8). Here from the beginning is exhibited this basic principle: all Christians share the evangelistic task but some Christians have a special gift of evangelism which God normally uses as his main instrument in evangelism. (See Acts 8:7, 12, 35 and 38 for the effectiveness of Philip and verse 25 for the ministry of the apostles.) A proper balance in emphasis between the general gift of witness-evangelism and the special gift of evangelism delivers us from unnecessary guilt (and jealousy) on the one hand and unthinkable 'opting-out' on the other.

Now it is true that the main agent of evangelism is the local church and that in the local church there will be several people with this gift — usually exercised informally. There is need, however, for the appointment by the wider church of those who have large gifts in evangelism who can strengthen the evangelistic outreach of the church.

This gift comes in an almost infinite variety of forms. Some are gifted in mass evangelism, others in personal evangelism. Some proclaim the message to children, others to adults. Some are most effective using drama, music, radio, television or letter writing. Some, like Calvin, are theologian-evangelists. Others like Wesley have a completely different gift mix (for example administrator-evangelist). Some may delight to door knock — others may specialise in evangelism which uses the gift of hospitality.

The important thing to emphasise is that each evangelist must develop his or her own style which is most consistent with the nature of the gospel and which is most appropriate to his or her personal call and gift mix.

Despite this variety in the expression of the gift of evangelism it is probably true that in the local church situation where there may not be great opportunity for specialising, those with a variety of forms of this gift will be able to co-operate in a single program of evangelism. That is, a person whose specialty is evangelistic preaching will probably be able to co- operate well in a program of home visiting.

Training courses in evangelism are important. Since every Christian has an evangelistic responsibility every Christian will profit from a course on evangelism. Such courses are especially important for those who have a special gift in this area.

Gift 4
Teacher
Ephesians 4:11

The last parish in which I served placed a great deal of emphasis on its teaching ministry. Two of its ministers and its pastoral elder (who was a full time member of staff) had teaching gifts. The two ministers had spent many years endeavouring to develop their teaching gifts. The delivery of teaching sermons in several of the six churches in the parish was given high priority in the weekly program. Some exciting growth occurred. Many new ministries were commenced. Many small groups met regularly throughout the parish. For several years the whole strategy of ministry in this parish centred around this teaching gift. Although not every parish should follow this pattern the teaching gift is important for the quality growth of every church.

The word teacher (*didaskalos*) occurs some fifty-nine times in the New Testament. Most of these references are in the gospels. The word refers to Jesus on forty-one occasions.

Jesus as the teacher

Jesus was regarded as a rabbi — a teacher of the law in Israel. Jesus was prophet-teacher; indeed *the* Prophet-Teacher. But even more than this, he spoke as Son of God. His 'I say to you' made him not merely the spokesman of God. He was God's mouth. It was not his teaching which was the crucial thing. It was his person. Authentic Christianity is not allegiance to the teaching of Jesus. It is allegiance to the person who is the teacher — and above that — who is the Saviour and Redeemer.

Christian teachers

(Acts 13:1; 1 Corinthians 12:28; Ephesians 4:11; James 3:1; 1 Timothy 2:7; 2 Timothy 1:11.)

In Acts 13:1 certain leaders in the church at Antioch had a combined gift of prophet-teacher. The prophet brought a direct word from God on specific issues. The teacher taught from the

34

scriptural tradition of the past. Teaching, like prophecy is a spiritual gift, not simply a natural talent. It requires the on-going development of the spiritual life for its maximum use.

The prophet-teacher

The combined gift of prophecy-teaching may have been especially important in the early church before the completion of the apostolic and prophetic Scriptures. It may also be important today. The word which comes out of the past may be made specific and concrete by the word which is given in the present. The traditional word of the teacher is made more contemporary by the inspired word of the prophet.

Just as the teacher needs the prophet, the prophet needs the teacher. In the apostolic church the teacher is essentially the teacher of Scripture. When the church strays from the witness of the apostles to Christ as contained in Scripture the church ceases to be apostolic and (therefore) Christian. It is probably true that since the completion of the apostolic (and prophetic) New Testament Scripture the teaching gift which has been given to certain members of the body of Christ has assumed a position of enormous importance.

There must never be a clash between the word of the prophet and the word of the teacher. The Spirit who gives both gifts is not the author of confusion. Both gifts must be consistent with Scripture and normally based on Scripture. Thus prophetic and teaching roles of the church are never in irreconcilable tension. The essential harmony of these two gifts is seen in the fact that from the beginning they have often been seen together in the same individuals.

The teaching gift is essential if the church is to remain apostolic. The teacher teaches the whole counsel of God. The teacher gives to the church its broad understanding of God's will and purposes. Above all, he or she teaches 'the teaching of the apostles'.

If the teacher unveils the whole painting the prophet focuses on very specific aspects of the picture.

If the teacher relies on preparation and study and learning, the prophet relies on inspiration. If the teacher gives us the whole, the prophet gives us the particular.

If, however, the part becomes separated from the whole (and the prophet dispenses with the teacher) prophecy becomes false prophecy.

The pastor-teacher

If teaching and prophecy are a common gift mix, so are teaching-pastoring.

Ephesians 4:11 speaks of 'some pastors and teachers'. The fact that the word 'some' does not appear before 'teacher' has led many commentators to assume that one person is being described — a person who has a combined gift of pastor-teacher.

The pastor-teacher was probably the person who led the local congregation. We may make the following observations:

The pastor-teacher pastors *through* teaching as well as in other ways.

The teacher who has a pastoral gift has a great understanding of, and sensitivity to, the flock. The pastoral gift keeps the teaching gift relevant.

Whereas the teaching gift is somewhat content centred (majoring on what is taught) the pastoral gift is person centred (majoring on who is taught). This double combination in the leader of the local church is highly beneficial for the building up of the congregation.

The teaching gift is not always accompanied by a pastoral gift. The parish is foolish to expect that every minister should have a special gift of pastoring. Nor does every pastor have a special teaching gift. We assume that in the sovereignty of the Spirit it is better that this variety should exist. Provided there are other parish staff, elders or other church members who have the missing gift, it is not necessary that the pastor should always be a teacher (and vice versa).

The scholar-teacher

Another common combination appears to be teaching-knowledge. The member of the body, who has the gift of 'the word of knowledge' is the person who has a special ability to understand, accumulate and share Christian (especially biblical) truth in such a way that the body is built up in the knowledge of God.

The person who has a teaching gift as well as a knowledge gift often becomes a scholar-teacher. It appears, however, that a person may have a teaching gift without a special gift of knowledge[9]. It is also possible to have a knowledge gift and perhaps become a great scholar in the church but not have the ability to communicate that knowledge readily or clearly. A person with a teaching gift is often able to take the great contribution of scholars who may have only the gift of knowledge and simplify and share that knowledge with the wider church.

The church of our day is often poverty-stricken in terms of knowledge because those of its scholars who have deep insight into God's truth but who may be unable to communicate with ordinary church members are dismissed as irrelevant. It is up to the teachers in the church to draw on the knowledge of its spiritually gifted scholars and to convey their insights to the wider church.

Practical considerations

If you realise you have a teaching gift — and especially if this is confirmed by the church, what should you do about it?

1 You should give yourself to your teaching. The emphasis in many places in the New Testament where gifts are spoken of is on the importance of concentrating on one's gift. Paul says: 'Having gifts that differ according to the grace given to us, let us use them . . . he who teaches, in his teaching' (Romans 12:6-7).

2 You should give yourself to training. A teaching gift must be developed. Practice (which we have just considered) and training are essential. Fortunately all kinds of courses in teaching method and Christian doctrine are available.

In many ways the more one prepares oneself the more inadequate one feels. And that is the way it should be. We are, however, speaking of a grace gift. We always remain dependent on grace. Do not, therefore, wait until you are fully trained before you exercise your gift. Exercise it where you are and as you are. But be prepared to develop your gift to the maximum so that your teaching will be worthy of the gospel and of the teacher who is our master and whose disciples we are.

3 'Take heed to yourself' (1 Timothy 4:16). The Christian faith is not so much taught as caught. Teaching is a spiritual gift — not a natural talent. The person who exercises this spiritual gift needs to live by the Spirit and develop the fruit of the Spirit. She or he needs to be a person of prayer relying on the Spirit of God for effective, fruitful communication.

The prime task of the Christian teacher is to be Christian. I am not first of all a teacher. I am primarily a disciple. What I am is more important than what I say. What I am will be communicated more effectively than what I formally teach.

So, let me give heed to myself as well as to my teaching.

4 You should expect to be fruitful. Normally the sign of a spiritual gift of teaching is that when it is exercised people learn.

It is important to assess the effectiveness of any ministry we are involved in. A false spirituality may drive us to stick at a ministry for which we have no special gift but for which someone else is very gifted.

If Sunday school teaching is a frustration to you, the childen do not readily learn and you find little fulfilment in it the reason may be that you are in the wrong ministry. (Of course you may be lacking in prayer, preparation or training. Or you may have a teaching gift which is more effective with adults than with children.) Prayerfully consider what are your best gifts and where they may most effectively be used. If you have a gift for the ministry in which you are involved and a calling to it then expect to be fruitful as you do it in the power of God's Spirit.

Gift 5
Pastor
Ephesians 4:11

At heart John Bellamy was a pastor. As an ordained minister he identified with his people in long-term commitment to them. He had served in a number of parishes and still prayed regularly for every congregation he had served. He loved to visit his people in his own parish, to listen to them unburden themselves and to serve them in any way he could.

Although without a special teaching gift, he had applied himself to preaching because he realised that the most important way by which he could pastor his people was through the ministry of the Word.[10] He had been ordained to the ministry of the Word and sacraments but for a considerable time did not realise that the ministry of the Word was the essence of his pastoral ministry. He had felt himself to be under tension. Not being a scholar or teacher by inclination he usually left his preaching preparation till the last minute. As much prime time as possible was spent on pastoral visiting and pastoral counselling.

Now he has a much more integrated view of his ministry. He has discovered that his gift mix is pastoring-exhortation. Pastoring is his largest gift but he realises that his secondary gift of exhortation constantly supports his main pastoring gift (through the ministry of encouragement). He is much more relaxed in his ministry now since he realised that it is as a Minister of the Word that he exercises his gifts. He spends some time each morning wherever possible in preparing himself through Bible study and prayer and in preparing his Sunday message. Sunday by Sunday he pastors the people through a biblical message of encouragement (exhortation).

What he has also found is that his daily preparation is of infinite value as he ministers the Word in his daily home visits. Although in these visits he often finds himself in a counselling situation and finds the insights from his training in psychology to be very helpful he nevertheless is increasingly realising that as a pastor the best way he can build up his people in this face to face situation is by the ministry of the Word.

John Roberts is the minister of a rapidly growing parish. He has a large pastoral gift and was rapidly heading toward burn-out as he tried to give himself to increasing leadership responsibilities and to keep up an extensive visitation program. He was rescued however, by spiritual gifts teaching. He now exercises his pastoral gift through preaching, pastoring the leaders of the church and in crisis counselling. He leaves the general visiting to the elders and another ordained minister who has been especially appointed to the parish staff to visit and to co-ordinate general visiting by elders and others who have pastoral gifts.

The pastor in the New Testament

The Greek word for pastor, *poimen*, means literally, shepherd. Only once (Ephesians 4:11) in the New Testament are congregational leaders spoken of as pastors. Jeremias, a famous New Testament scholar thinks that in this passage 'pastor' is not yet an established title. These shepherds are leaders of the local church. They may be called pastors or shepherds (Ephesians 4:11) or presbyters or elders (*presbuteroi* 1 Peter 5:1) and sometimes bishops (*episkopoi* 1 Timothy 3:1). These terms appear to be generally interchangeable. Jeremias suggests that the task of the pastor was to care for the congregation (Acts 20:28; 1 Peter 5:2-4), seek the lost (Matthew 18:12-14) and combat heresy (Acts 20:29f).[11]

The pattern for every pastor is Jesus the Good Shepherd (John 10:1-30). His first function was to gather the lost sheep of Israel (Matthew 9:36) although his concern reaches much beyond this (John 10:16). In order to save the lost sheep he must die and rise again for them (Matthew 26:31f). The climax of this in-gathering will be the Day of Judgement when the goats will be separated from the sheep. We can say, then, that in order to exercise a pastoral gift one must follow the example of Jesus especially in caring for the flock (even being willing to lay down one's life for the sheep) and in developing a close relationship with each sheep.

The pastor serves as under-shepherd with Christ as the Chief Shepherd and model. The pastor's commitment to the 'flock' is a long-term one. His or her task consists in general care of the group with special attention to any who are straying and to any source of heresy.

It is paradoxical that not all pastors (ministers) have a special pastoral gift. Sometimes this gift is over-emphasized by parish members. Gifted pastors tend to be very popular with their flock and there can be strong reaction against a new minister who does not appear to be skilled in pastoral work. He or she may appear remote from the people.[12]

Parishes must be open to the virtual certainty that there will be lay people in every parish to whom the Spirit of God has given the pastoral gift. Some of these lay people should be appointed to the office of eldership, although we must not assume that every elder will have a pastoral gift. Some church members will exercise their pastoral gifts in the way in which most gifts are exercised, i.e. informally and without holding a special office in the parish.

The person who holds the office of pastor (the parish minister) is often the key to the growth of the church. This will often mean that he or she cannot spend a great deal of time in pastoral visiting but must concentrate on leadership responsibilities including planning for church growth. The gifts of faith and leadership are probably of much more importance in such a parish minister than the gift of pastor. In some cases a parish can sustain two Ministers, one of whom can concentrate on leadership responsibilities. If the other minister has a pastoral gift he or she may lead the pastoral team of lay visitors in the parish pastoral ministry.

The big failing of many ministers is that they attempt to be omni-competent in order to fulfil the wishes of parish members, and also to fulfil their concept of a pastor. The result can be tragi-comic for all concerned. Such a person tries to be *the* teacher (knowledgeable on every subject and angry or hurt if his or her competence is questioned) and pastor for all occasions.

The leadership role of the pastor is vital. This must mean an acceptance of the need to think, to dream and to share the thinking and dreaming with others so that the whole body may be involved in ministry.

In this section we have been thinking of the special gift of pastoring in terms of a special ability which some Christians have of long-term nurturing of a group of Christians in the faith. It is probable that in Scripture there is another important use of the concept of pastoring or shepherding . This refers to the function of leadership. In many places in the Bible leaders are called shepherds. Indeed shepherds lead their flock. In this sense all Ministers are pastors (leading the flock) but they do not necessarily possess a special pastoral gift which we usually associate with pastoral visitation.

41

Where it is assumed that the minister is the only person with a pastoral gift the growth of the church will generally plateau off when the membership reaches the number of families which the minister feels he or she can pastor. Unconsciously the minister will defend him or herself against further growth because he or she cannot effectively pastor more than (say) one hundred families. This may be one of the reasons why many Australian churches stop growing when the effective membeship reaches 100-200. This situation is somewhat relieved in the case of the minister who has a pastoring-teaching gift mix. He or she can actually do a good deal of effective pastoring through his or her teaching. This means that to some extent the minister can pastor an unlimited number of members. These members, however, will from time to time need face-to-face counselling as they meet particular problems and crises in their lives. Much of this individual counselling can be done by the associate minister (where there is one) and by elders and others with pastoral and other appropriate gifts. The leading minister where he or she has a pastoral gift, may be contacted in the case of particularly difficult pastoral problems.

If the Australian church is to win a significant number of Australians to Christ and into his church then its ministers must increasingly be freed to give themselves to leadership, oversight and planning. The bulk of face-to-face pastoring will have to be carried out by others in the congregation who are gifted for it. In other words ministers will have to be pastors in the leadership sense rather than pastors in the sense of the nurturing of individuals.

Questions If it is true that there is no gift without a corresponding ministry, what is the obligation on individuals who have a pastoral gift and on the parishes to which they belong?

(Keep in mind the possibility of informal ministries.)

Should denominations (for example the Uniting Church) increasingly make provision for long-term pastoral ministries in situations where the relationship between the (pastoral) minister and people is close and healthy — thus allowing the fullest possible exercise of the long-term commitment nature of the pastor's gift? What could be the advantages and disadvantages of making such a provision?

Gift 6
Exhortation
Romans 12:8

The Greek word *parakaleo* is made up of *kaleo* 'to call' and *para* 'to the side' and means literally 'to call to one's side'. It is related to the word for the Holy Spirit (*paraclete*) which conveys the idea that the Spirit is the one who is called to one's side. He is our helper-strengthener, encourager and comforter. To exhort (*parakaleo*) means to beg or urge, to encourage, request, console, comfort and cheer up.

Barnabas in Acts is like a comet which flashes across the sky for a brief time giving light until it disappears from view. Barnabas is not one of the bright stars of Acts. But he does bring light. Indeed his light sparkles for he is a very attractive character. He is the Son of Encouragement (Acts 4:36).

By his ministry of exhortation-encouragement he assisted others to go on walking in the light. Barnabas was responsible for drawing the converted Paul into the circle of disciples (Acts 9:27).

We might be surprised to realise what influence those who have the gift of encouragement have on the life and spirit of the church — and therefore on its growth. It is perhaps the tendency of most of us to give up on people — to expect the worst of them — to be pessimists. Those who have a gift of exhortation put their arm around those whom we push away from us. They push them on where we might put them down.

Barnabas was no great man. In the church missionary story he is completely overshadowed by Paul. But he, like Andrew (John 1:40f) found a famous 'brother'. If he achieved no more than that — and he accomplished much more than that — his life would have been well spent. Greatness does not consist in lighting a candle for yourself, but in preventing the flickering candle of another from extinguishing.

In Acts 11, we read that the Christians were scattered following persecution which arose over Stephen. At first, the gospel was shared only with Jews. But at Antioch some Greeks believed (verses 19-20). When news of this came to Jerusalem action had to be taken. It was important that should this be a genuine work of the Spirit it be acknowledged as such by the apostolic Jerusalem church. There should be no separate non-apostolic church. No doubt some Jerusalem Jewish Christians were uneasy about this new departure into Gentile evangelism. In the providence of God no better person could have been chosen than Barnabas to enquire into the development at Antioch.

Barnabas, it seems, was an open and positive person — always eager to see the grace of God in others. He was an optimistic man of faith. Having received the comfort and encouragement of the Spirit he was able to encourage others. We read 'When he came and saw the grace of God, he was glad' (verse 23). No Jewish prejudice kept him from recognising the grace of God. We read again: 'and he exhorted them all to remain faithful to the Lord with steadfast purpose; for he was a good man, full of the Holy Spirit and of faith. And a large company was added to the Lord' (verses 23-24). We note the following.

1 No doubt the joy which Barnabas received inspired him in his ministry to the Christians at Antioch. It may be that joy is a characteristic of the person who has a gift of exhortation.

2 Barnabas' gift of exhortation was of particular help in what we would call 'follow-up'. It may be that this gift is of particular importance in assisting new converts and in the work of nurture following evangelism.

3 He was full of the Holy Spirit. His exhortation was true charisma. We need to go on being filled with the Spirit (Ephesians 5:18) if we are to use our gifts to the full!

4 Barnabas was also full of faith. It is of the nature of faith to be optimistic — to be open to the grace of God in others; to accept them and affirm them and encourage them. Again we notice that the work of exhortation like that of other gifts is not of human origin. It is a work of God. It requires faith.

5 We read that a large company was added to the Lord (Acts 11:24). It appears that the gift of exhortation may have an enormous evangelistic impact. Why were people won in this situation? We can only guess. Was it that the confidence and assurance of the new converts — as a result of Barnabas' exhortation ministry — attracted outsiders to the church's message? Did the ministry of encouragement give the new

converts evangelistic courage?. Did Barnabas exercise his ministry of encouragement to the outsiders as well as the insiders?

Probably all of these were factors in the movement of the Spirit of God at that particular time.

It is interesting to note that Luke goes on immediately to say: 'So Barnabas went to Tarsus to look for Saul; and when he had found him, he brought him to Antioch' (Acts 11:26). We have not heard of Paul since chapter nine. He apparently had spent a silent period of isolation in the city of his birth. But Barnabas had not forgotten him. He was not likely to allow such talent to be buried in the ground. (Is it possible that there was still some hesitancy about Paul in the eyes of some who knew him formerly as an arch-enemy of the church?) Barnabas could have jealously guarded his leadership role at Antioch. He knew however that Paul had the right gifts and that the church at Antioch needed him. A self-centred defensive spirit would keep him from playing second-fiddle and the kingdom of God from advancing. (Does a defensive spirit sometimes keep us from acknowledging and affirming the gifts of others?)

This chapter concludes with Barnabas and Saul returning to Judea with a love gift from the church at Antioch. We can imagine that Barnabas went on this errand enthusiastically. He had joy in doing anything which would affirm or encourage his brothers and sisters in Christ. We see in Barnabas that the gift of exhortation, although primarily a speaking gift, is also expressed in terms of action and loving service.

People like Barnabas are beautiful people but they can be awkward in a Parish Council! They will not let go — especially if they think they may be able to help a weak brother or sister. Silas is the obvious choice for Parish Council secretary. Why risk everything by appointing Mark (Acts 15:37)?

There is nothing in the text to say whether Paul or Barnabas was correct. (Paul did receive the blessing of the church. Acts 15:40) In the providence of God both missions (that of Paul and Silas and that of Barnabas and Mark) were successful.

Perhaps the Spirit of God turned the dispute (which was over a matter of opinion rather than of principle) to all-round advantage. In the end Barnabas' gamble seems justified. But Mark could easily have failed and thereby placed in jeopardy the whole mission. John Mark proved himself and later became the author of the gospel which has made him much more famous and influential in the ongoing life of the church than a thousand Barnabases.

The truth of this last statement, of course, depends on how you look at it. Who is behind Mark's Gospel and all the letters of Paul? Perhaps without Barnabas and his gift of encouragement, a third of the New Testament would not have been written.

Both Timothy and Titus were involved in a ministry of exhortation. It may be that all who like them have oversight of congregations must (to some considerable extent) exercise this ministry.

Timothy is exhorted not to rebuke the older man (literally 'a father') but to exhort him (parakalei 1 Timothy 5:1). Exhortation is sharply distinguished from rebuke. Rebuke is far less positive and may break and discourage an older person. It was inappropriate in that society for a young man like Timothy to appear to pass judgement on an old person who was perhaps acknowledged as a leader in the community. But exhortation — encouragement — was entirely appropriate.

Part of Timothy's ministry of the Word was ongoing exhortation: 'preach the word . . . convince, rebuke and exhort . . .' (2 Timothy 4:2).[13]

Titus is exhorted to urge (parakalei) the younger men to control themselves (Titus 2:6). He is told: 'Declare these things; exhort and reprove (or rebuke) with all authority. Let no one disregard you' (2:15). Both the ministry of exhortation as well as that of rebuke is to be carried out with all authority. Clearly the exhorter speaks not on his or her own authority, but on behalf of God and with his authority.

Exhortation is not only an important ministry for those who have oversight of local congregations. It is part of the ministry of every Christian although, no doubt, it is a particular responsibility for those who have a special exhortation gift (Romans 12:8). The writer of Hebrews emphasises the need for every Christian to exercise constantly whatever gift of exhortation he or she may have: 'But exhort one another every day . . . that none of you may be hardened by the deceitfulness of sin' (3:13). In a passage which itself is pure exhortation, the writer of Hebrews exhorts his readers (as well as himself) to encourage one another, especially as they see the coming of Christ drawing near (10:25).

The gift of exhortation today

It will be readily seen that a very important means by which this

46

gift (either general or special) is exercised is through preaching. It is in preaching that the congregation can be urged and encouraged in the light of the past and future salvation in Christ. It is in preaching that the pastor and prophet can apply the written word and encourage the struggling church to go forward with joy.

All who preach — all who pastor or prophesy will need to beseech and encourage their congregations — both publicly and privately (face to face). Anyone who has a gift of exhortation — encouragement (whether male or female) might well consider becoming a preacher. This gift, however, can be exercised not only in public where application of the Word is necessarily general. It may be used in private to assist a particular person who has a specific problem.

Exhortation, then, may be of great value in the counselling situation whether the counselling be directive or non-directive. Thus a person who has a large special gift of exhortation might well consider becoming a counsellor of some kind. Indeed he or she may fulfil both a preaching and counselling role.

It appears obvious that the person who is attracted to both preaching and counselling might well consider the ordained ministry where both roles can be easily combined. On the other hand the Australian church appears to be in desperate need of appointing full-time lay or ordained Christian counsellors to the staffs of larger churches or parishes. These persons may well also preach from time to time. As we have seen the person who has a pastoral gift may often have this gift as well. If not, he or she will have to be content to operate on a general gift of exhortation. The pastor cannot get by without exercising this gift to some extent.

Often there are gifted and trained people within the congregation who can take on the time-consuming, but essential, work of on-going counselling. The minister in a single-minister parish, even if he or she has this gift (or some other appropriate special gift which can be used in counselling), should probably not spend too much time in personal counselling. He or she may have to be content with exercising this gift mainly through preaching (and perhaps amongst the elders on a one-to-one basis).

Gift 7
The word of wisdom
1 Corinthians 12:8

This morning Wilma stayed behind after the support group. She suggested that the committee members of the Foundation, which supports my ministry, should meet together informally a couple of times a year — that this should be in addition to regular business meetings and that members' spouses should be invited. She felt that in the informality of fellowship over a meal our ministry would be strengthened. She also made another important suggestion which had all the marks of divine wisdom on it.

Wilma recently became an elder. Her contribution to the life of the parish is recognised. What makes her gift especially effective is her dedication to Christ. She is a woman of prayer. Her wisdom is not simply a natural talent. It is a spiritual gift. What is perhaps most significant is that Wilma is a gifted teacher of God's Word. She is particularly gifted in sharing God's Word with children. But she is also a helpful preacher.

I suggest that the word of wisdom is particularly important in the proclamation of the Word, both in preaching and less formal ways. Its function in the church meeting and in offering a specific word of practical guidance is secondary to this and is indeed the outcome of it.

The word of wisdom ensures that the gospel will go on being proclaimed effectively against all difficulties — and that its message will be communicated in the most convincing way. How helpful this gift is in a Parish or Elders' Council. It can keep the church from going off on tangents. It can deliver the church from frustration, bring together various points of view, and save the church from wasted effort and spiritual and emotional stress. It does this by pointing the church in the right direction — to the way of the cross.

Wisdom is particularly needed to complement the gift of faith. Faith brings vision but wisdom brings direction. Wisdom refines vision. Wisdom also complements knowledge. It shows us how knowledge should be applied. It tells us what knowledge is relevant to a particular complex situation. It shows us the way ahead — often selecting the best way from several alternatives. In order to do this, wisdom must know the destination — it must have its priorities right. Its first concern must be the kingdom of God. It must be centred in Christ. Otherwise it will merely display human wisdom — perhaps a talent of wisdom, but certainly not a gift of wisdom which speaks a word from above, i.e. a gift of a word of wisdom.

In 1 Corinthians true wisdom is radically different from the world's wisdom (1:18-19, 26-27; 3:19). It does not originate with humankind but with the Spirit (2:4,10). It is not a matter of eloquent or plausible words or of human philosophy (1:17; 2:1,4). It is centred in the cross of Christ (1:17). Indeed Christ himself is the embodiment of wisdom (1:30). This wisdom which comes from above is a matter of revelation and saving power (1:18, 24). It is secret, hidden and eternal wisdom (2:7). It is irreconcilable with a divisive (3:1-7) or proud (3:18-23) spirit.

It is probably better to see this gift not so much in terms of a sudden miraculous giving of wisdom but a settled attitude of mind which is inspired by God's Spirit and which has a comprehensive understanding of God's purposes as revealed in Scripture, as centred in the crucified Christ and as leading to the Christlike life.[14]

Jesus is the supreme example of one who possessed this gift. He was always able, for example, to answer with skill the trick questions of the Pharisees. His answers which exposed the folly of the Pharisees are always related to God's purpose in himself as Messiah.

Stephen also possessed this gift. He was chosen as a deacon partly because he had this gift (Acts 6:3). From 6:14 and 7:25 we see that Stephen's message of wisdom was centred in Christ and majored in the gospel.

There is a danger in seeing this gift as the ability to utter wise infallible sayings which are short-cuts to problem-solving and do away with the need for responsible leadership and long-term careful planning.

Misunderstanding the gifts of knowledge and wisdom — a warning

An error into which we may easily fall in our emphasis on spiritual gifts is the Corinthian error. A group of elite charismatic

Christians at Corinth claimed special gifts of knowledge which set them apart from, and above, the body. This special wisdom and knowledge gave them power over (and above) others in the body and made them proud. This knowledge and wisdom was cut-off (abstracted) from Christ, his cross and Christian living. To focus exclusively on special insights and special guidance when interpreting these gifts is no doubt to trivialize them. They are much larger than the Corinthians understood them to be. Their main purpose was not so much to provide esoteric hidden knowledge and wisdom to a few but to assist in the communication to all of the gospel which had been revealed. The special insights and special guidance which are, no doubt, also expressions of these same gifts are the outcome of, and related to, the proclamation of the gospel. The knowledge and wisdom are centred in Christ, result in practical Christian living and lead to the effective proclamation of the Word of the gospel. These are gospel, and therefore, proclamation, gifts.

Gift 8
The word of knowledge
1 Corinthians 12:8

I consider that my first gift-mix is probably pastoring-teaching-knowledge. As a young teenager, I began to take an interest in theology. Since candidating for the ministry I have spent many years in theological and biblical studies. I think that I have learned one thing well: how little we really do know! (Paul who no doubt had this gift in abundant measure, said 'now we see in a mirror dimly'. 1 Corinthians 13:12) I am constantly reminded of how inadequate all those years of study have been. I do not see my knowledge gift as a particularly large one. I am, I think, essentially a pastor-teacher. Knowledge however serves my teaching gift.

The biblical teaching on knowledge

In the Old Testament, the knowledge of God is always linked with God's acts of self-revelation.[15] When God says 'And you shall know that I am the Lord (Yahweh)' it is always linked with a specific *act* of the Lord. See, for example, Ezekiel 11:10.

Testimony to God's past actions (Exodus 10:1-2) and special signs lead to the knowledge of God. The knowledge of God in the Old Testament had nothing to do with speculative questions about God. It had to do with God revealing himself to humanity. To know God means entering into the personal relationship which he himself makes possible.

Knowledge of God involves doing justice and righteousness (Jeremiah 22:15-16).

Knowledge in the Old Testament, then, is quite a different thing from that in Greek literature where it refers to detached and speculative knowledge. In Hebrew thought, knowledge always comes out of personal encounter with the God who reveals himself.

Knowledge in the New Testament is not something which is purely theoretical. Phrases like knowing the law (Romans 7:1)

51

and knowing God's will (Romans 2:18) do not imply a theoretical knowledge, but personal knowledge which demands obedience.

When the New Testament speaks of God's knowledge, it reflects the Old Testament usage. It refers, for example, to God's loving, electing knowledge of humanity (2 Timothy 2:19; 1 Corinthians 8:3; 13:12; Galatians 4:9). This knowledge, again, leads to personal relationship — i.e. to the knowledge of God himself, as revealed in Jesus Christ (2 Corinthians 2:14; 4:6).

There are two interpretations of this gift.

1 A word of revelation from God. This interpretation may be based on such verses as 1 Corinthians 13:2 and 14:6 or on John 4:17-18 and Acts 5:3,9. Such a gift would be especially helpful in Christian counselling.[16]

2 The ability to speak with knowledge. Understood in this way the gift of knowledge is the special facility which is given to some Christians to understand and absorb a profound knowledge of the Word of God and to share it with others. It is frequently related to the teaching gift and is an important gift for the Christian scholar.

I prefer to understand this gift in the second sense and to see what is described under 1 above as referring to an aspect of the prophetic gift.[17]

Conclusion

However we define this gift, it must never be cut off from the knowledge of God in Christ or from practical Christian living. Nor must it concentrate on special knowledge which makes people proud.

It appears to me that there are those who have a gift of knowledge without a corresponding gift of teaching. (See explanation given in Gift 4, Teacher, above.)

Knowledge without discernment is of little value. Let us examine the gift of discernment seeing how necessary it is for a proper functioning not only of knowledge but of all the gifts.

Gift 9
Discernment
1 Corinthians 12:10

The church of Christ is a dynamic organism where the Spirit of God is active. All the gifts are given and used. This apostolic church is above all prophetic.

Wherever there is prophecy there is likely to be false prophecy. Anyone can claim to have a message from God. Speaking in tongues is not always an indication of the presence of the Spirit. Those who claim to bring a word of knowledge or of wisdom may be mistaken.

In the context of speaking about spiritual gifts Paul emphasises our limited ability in this age to discern God's truth. He says, 'We see in a mirror dimly' (1 Corinthians 13:12). Paul here is teaching that even those with such gifts as prophecy and faith find it hard to see clearly God's will and truth. We are prone to make mistakes. Our clearest prophetic visions (Acts 2:17) are blurred. If we are to discern the mind of God with any accuracy at all then we shall need the varying insights which come from the varying gifts. But above all we shall need the discernment which the Spirit of God gives to the church through the special gift of discernment. Without this gift the gifted church will fall victim to all kinds of extremes, erratic ministries, false teaching, immaturity in behaviour and witness, and division.

The biblical teaching

In 1 Corinthians 12 the complementary nature of the gifts is stressed. The tendency of the Corinthians was to focus on the spectacular, miraculous gifts, especially on tongues. If the unity and good order (14:40) of the church is to be preserved then the gift of discernment will be needed.

The gift of discernment here appears between prophecy and speaking in tongues. Paul places great emphasis on prophecy (14:1) but realizes that its function is limited (13:9-10). What the prophets say must be checked (14:29). Tongues also may get out of hand. The person with the gift of discernment may often be able to discriminate between what is false prophecy and what is authentic, and between genuine and counterfeit tongues. He or she may also be able to discriminate between the brother or sister who has something to say and the one who has to say something!

Exorcism requires discernment and should not be exercised without it. [18]

The New Testament makes it clear that it is not easy to distinguish between the spirits. The fact that a person speaks with enthusiasm, ecstacy or charisma does not guarantee that what he or she says comes from the Spirit. Even the fact that a person has a recognised gift of faith, knowledge, wisdom or prophecy does not guarantee what that person always says is wholly helpful. Continuous discernment is needed.

It is possible that the gift of discernment may relate to:

message
motive
behaviour.

1 Corinthians 12:10 is literally 'discernings of spirits' and may emphasise the variety of forms of this gift. [19]

Where prophecy is concerned the emphasis will, no doubt, be on the ability to distinguish between the prophetic message which comes from the Holy Spirit and that which comes from a false spirit.

Some with the gift of discernment may be able to discern genuine from false motives. Because of the warning of Christ we must be careful about developing a judging spirit (Matthew 7:1). But discernment is needed (Matthew 7:6).

Paul apparently exercised this gift in the case of Ananias and Sapphira (Acts 5:1-10) and in the case of Simon the sorcerer (Acts 8:22-23).

In Acts 16:16-18, Paul showed a gift of discernment when he identified particular behaviour as indicative of demon possession. In this passage discernment and exorcism are twin gifts.

In a day when the cults are flourishing because of the vacuum created by materialism, secularism, theological liberalism, biblical illiteracy and dead orthodoxy a charismatic renewal (note the small 'c') appears to offer hope for the recovery of New Testament Christianity. Unless this movement is accompanied, however, by discernment of spirits it may well dissipate in undisciplined, undiscerning and divisive extremism.

Questions According to 1 John 4:1-7 and Matthew 7:15-22, what are some of the tests which can be applied to see whether or not a prophet is false?

Other tests which are not listed in this passage are:

Does he or she submit to church leadership? (Hebrews 13:17; 1 Corinthians 14:37)

Does he or she speak for too long? (1 Corinthians 14:29-30)

Does he or she submit to Scripture? (Matthew 22:29)[20]

Can you add to this list?

How can we strike the proper balance between discerning false teaching and indulging in heresy hunting?

Gift 10
Missionary

We have seen that *the* basic gift in the life of the church is that of apostleship. I have argued that this gift in its primary form resided in the original apostles and that today it resides in the whole church which is apostolic when it is faithful to the apostolic message and mission concerning Christ. I have also argued that in a secondary sense particular leaders in the church may have an apostolic gift.

I have also suggested that apostolic functions are performed by those who have the gift of evangelism. I want to suggest here the possibility that the gift of missionary was given to the church in order to take the gospel into cross-cultural situations. In other words we may say that as the church grew and the apostles died the mission function of the original apostles was performed increasingly by evangelists and missionaries. Some of the original apostles (like Peter) served mainly their own culture while some (like Paul, Ephesians 3:6-8) proclaimed the message in a cross-cultural situation. The missionary fulfils the function of the latter type of apostle.

If this analysis is correct then the gift of missionary is (like evangelist) directly related to the basic gift in the church — that of apostle.

If the church is to be the true apostolic church of Christ it must be a missionary church. It follows that if the 2,400 million 'hidden people' in the world are to hear the gospel in our day then missionaries (together with evangelists) will be the main means through which they will hear it.[21] Only some members of the body have this special gift but all should have a general missionary concern. We describe those who have the general missionary gift as 'world Christians'.[22]

It is the God-given commission for every Christian and every congregation to have as a primary concern the winning of the nations to Christ. Let all Australian churches (including Uniting Churches) give priority in all their planning, budgeting, praying and programming to raising up missionaries, to supplying vital missionary information and to giving ongoing mission support. Only then will the church be truly apostolic and truly Christian.

Although I favour the view which sees 'missionary' as one of the key (apostolic) gifts, another view which is possible is that 'missionary' is a special calling rather than a specific gift. This assumes that it may not require a special charisma to serve in a cross-cultural situation. In this case a special call to missionary service would involve:

a call to full-time service
guidance to the place of service.

Gift 11
Courage (Martyrdom)
1 Corinthians 13:3

Although the evidence for a gift (charisma) of martyrdom is not conclusive it may be supported on the following grounds.

1 1 Corinthians 13:3 speaks of delivering one's body to be burned. Although this appears to be a clear reference to martyrdom no commentary on 1 Corinthians which I have consulted suggests that this is a gift (charisma) of martyrdom to which Paul is referring.[23] Although several spiritual gifts are referred to in this chapter many scholars argue that it was separately written and (appropriately) inserted here to support Paul's argument. If this is true, it may be incorrect to see each phrase in verses 1-3 and 8-9 as referring to specific gifts. That was perhaps not its original purpose.

   On the other hand the scholars may have generally failed to appreciate how integral 1 Corinthians 13 is to the whole context. Interpreting each phrase in these verses as references to specific charismata may bring about a reinterpretation of 1 Corinthians 13 and a new appreciation of its unity within the context of 1 Corinthians. We conclude that it is just possible that Paul is referring to a charisma of martyrdom here but that the evidence is inconclusive.

2 Study of the history of Christian martyrs reveals the charismatic nature of these witnesses. They have shown forgiveness, peace, joy, endurance, courage and boldness in witness to a remarkable degree.[24] (See Acts 6:10,15; 7:55-60) Ignatius wrote of the basic ingredients in martyrdom: conflict with the Devil, identification with, and extension of, the sufferings of Christ, Christ's mysterious presence and the infilling of joy and power.[25]

3 As with other spiritual gifts this gift leads to the building up of the church (Acts 8:1). The blood of the martyrs has always been the seed of the church.

4 Some Christians seem to show extraordinary courage in the face of persecution and death, whereas other Christians of

similar dedication do not. Some Christians choose to remain in dangerous situations which lead to death whereas other dedicated Christians withdraw from such situations.

Questions Do you think that the above arguments constitute grounds for believing in a special gift of courage (martyrdom)?

Do you agree that there is a special ability which the Spirit of God gives to some Christians in special measure (and all Christians to some extent) to show great courage in the face of opposition and impending death?

Gift 12
Speaking in tongues
1 Corinthians 12:10

Graham is a Minister of the Word. For several years he has spoken in tongues in his own devotions. He does not make a big deal out of this but experiences great liberty and joy as he praises God directly. His supernatural speech seems to assist him to transcend the limitations of normal speech. He is quite sure that although many other Christians do not have this gift, it is for him a genuine gift which has been given to him by the Spirit of God.

I shall argue in what follows that the special gift of speaking in tongues is the special ability which some Christians have in our day as in New Testament times, to pray directly with God (spirit to Spirit) in an unknown tongue. It may also be true that some other Christians who do not have this special gift may from time to time under the sovereign Spirit speak in tongues. It is not a *necessary* sign of a second experience (subsequent to conversion) of the Holy Spirit. Although this gift may be counterfeited it should not be despised when it is a genuine gift of the Holy Spirit. It is not as important for the life of the church as many other gifts. It, like all the gifts, is secondary to the fruit of the Spirit. Its main value is to give the individual Christian a sense of liberty in the private prayer of praise. When used in church it must be accompanied by the gift of interpretation.

New Testament teaching on tongues

The gift of the Spirit at Pentecost came as a result of Christ's death-resurrection-ascension (John 7:39; 16:7). The new age of the Spirit — the age of the gospel and of the church — which began at Pentecost depended on the completed work of Christ on the cross (John 19:30).

To some extent the speaking in tongues on the Day of Pentecost was a unique sign. Later speaking in tongues required interpretation (1 Corinthians 14:27) whereas on the day of Pentecost this was not necessary (Acts 2:11).

Pentecost, however, was not only a unique event. It is a continuing experience. Every one who would become a Christian must go through the doorway which was opened at Pentecost. Everyone must be born again of the Spirit (John 3:3). Because of Christ's death and resurrection and the resulting gift of the Spirit the filling of the Spirit is available to every believer (Acts 2:17,18,38,39). Although we receive the Spirit of God in abundance when we become Christians we need to go on being filled with God's Spirit (Ephesians 5:18). We can make the following points about tongues in Acts and 1 Corinthians.

1 Although the gift of tongues at Pentecost had some unique features it is an ongoing gift in the life of the church. See 1 Corinthians 14:39. Tongues *will* cease but the reference in 1 Corinthians 13:8 is to the return of Christ. Till then, while we cannot dictate to the Spirit the church should remain open to tongues as a genuine spiritual gift.

2 Since Pentecost begins a new age we should not take the pre-Pentecost experience of the 120 disciples as the pattern to follow. (Before Pentecost they had believed. Later at Pentecost they received the baptism of the Spirit.) The pattern for us is the 3,000 who on the day of Pentecost both believed and received the gift of the Holy Spirit (Acts 2:38).

3 In the three occasions in Acts speaking in tongues is a church-founding, group experience and never the second experience of an individual.[26] In Acts 2:4; 10:46 and 19:6 there was a special circumstance which marked a new beginning in the spread of the gospel. Also in Acts no one ever *seeks* speaking in tongues. The gift was given by the sovereign Spirit.

4 Being an historical account Acts describes what happened and not what necessarily should happen. (It is descriptive rather than prescriptive.) In order to discover what is normative for us we should look to the teaching parts of Scripture (for example 1 Corinthians 12-14) rather than the historical sections (for example Acts). In 1 Corinthians speaking in tongues *is* an ongoing gift in the life of the church but it is not presented there as the sign of being filled or baptised with the Spirit.

5 In 1 Corinthians 12-14, as we have seen, tongues is a genuine gift of the Spirit (12:10) which is not as valuable as those gifts which build up the body (14:19). It is given like all other gifts, to some Christians only (12:30) although others may exercise it from time to time (14:5). It is of particular benefit in the praise of God in private devotions (14:16,28). Where it is exercised in church the principle of good order must prevail. An

interpretation must be given (14:13,40) and a limit placed on the number of those exercising the gift (14:27). Love (not tongues or any other gift) is the crowning virtue (12:31b; 13:13).

6 The tongues at Pentecost were accompanied by prophecy. Indeed there is a strong emphasis on both tongues (Acts 2:4,11) and especially prophecy. (Acts 2:17,18. Peter's whole sermon seems prophetic.)

It appears as though the dramatic events of Pentecost are saying, 'At the outset of the gospel-Spirit age Babel is reversed and all men and women may be re-united by the universal language of the gospel'. Perhaps it was the presence of the gift of prophecy along with that of tongues which made this possible.

7 The ongoing gift of tongues while not to be seen as an altogether different gift from that of Acts 2 does not seem to have this function of uniting diverse language groups. Its danger is that it may lead to confusion (1 Corinthians 14:16,22 and particularly 23).

8 If Paul appears in 1 Corinthians 12-14 to be putting the brakes on as far as the Corinthian charismatics were concerned perhaps in some of our churches today Paul would apply the accelerator!

If we are to remain open to all that the Spirit is offering his church today we need to heed the following principles.

1 'Do not forbid speaking in tongues' (1 Corinthians 14:39). The following must not become one of our official hymns!

Oh — you can't do that there 'ere;

No — you can't do that there 'ere;

Anywhere else you could do that there,

But you can't do that there 'ere.

Paul saw many wrong emphases in the carnal charismatic Corinthian church. But he strenuously refused to condemn speaking in tongues. He instructed the church to be open to this authentic gift of the Spirit.

Speaking in tongues *may* be Satanic and opposed to Christ (1 Corinthians 12:2-3). Glossolalia is not confined to Christendom. It may also be a merely psychological response to religious emotion. It may be artificially induced in a group where it is encouraged and expected and where it gives status in that group. The danger of counterfeiting the gift (by imitation) is

62

particularly strong if it is implied that those who do not speak in tongues are immature Christians who have not had the ultimate spiritual experience of baptism in the Spirit. Despite all these dangers we must not endeavour to be more Christian than Paul by resisting this gift altogether. A conservative spirit may not always reflect a biblical and Christian attitude. It may simply be Pharisaic — making void the Word of God which refuses to deny tongues as an authentic gift of the Spirit.

2 We must recognise that tongues is one gift among many and that it is not the most important one. Private speaking in tongues is not as important as gifts which contribute to the building up of the body. It is subservient to the fruit of the Spirit, especially hope and above all love.

3 Speaking in tongues is not the sign of a special experience of the Spirit which every Christian ought to have. Insisting that speaking in tongues is the sign of baptism in the Spirit (interpreted as a second experience after conversion) is inherently divisive because it creates first and second class Christians and because it tends to create spiritual pride and a sense of inferiority.

4 We must recognise that some Spirit-filled Christians never speak in tongues. It is possible that some Christians without a special gift of speaking in tongues may, under the sovereignty of God's Spirit, speak in tongues from time to time. This should not, however, be taken to indicate a special gift.

If Romans 8:26 refers to the general gift (which may or may not be accompanied by tongues) then there may be three groups of Spirit filled Christians (none more advanced than the other) all of whom constantly experience the truth of Romans 8:26:

Those who sometimes speak in tongues but who have no special gift.

Those who never speak in tongues.

Those with a special gift of tongues and who regularly exercise it.[27]

5 We need to recognise that from a positive point of view speaking (or singing) in tongues assists the person with this gift to communicate with and praise God with great freedom unhindered by the restrictions of one's native language and by the restrictions of the mind. What is spoken is unfettered by the censorship of reason. It reflects the mind of the Spirit and the

will of God. Rational thought is by-passed as spirit communes with Spirit. Tongues may also provide emotional release (catharsis) and may be a means of glorifying God. Several movements (particularly among drug addicts) seem to have been accompanied by this gift.

6 Every attempt by theologians like B. B. Warfield to demonstrate that the gift of tongues belonged only to the apostolic age and gradually ceased with the closing of that age cannot be sustained. They seem arbitrary interpretations. Not originating in the Bible they are imposed on the Bible. Many Christians deny their own principle of biblical authority by ruling out tongues. Paul's only quarrel with the Corinthian tongues speakers was over the abuse of tongues in the assembly. We must beware lest we make void the word of God by our own traditions even if they are evangelical ones!

If you have a genuine special gift of speaking in tongues be thankful for it and exercise it in humility, freedom and joy to the glory of God.

Question In respect of tongues and other gifts is your church in need of a brake or an accelerator?

Gift 13
Interpretation of tongues
1 Corinthians 12:10, 30; 14:13, 27, 28

It would appear that the main function of speaking in tongues is for the purpose of private prayer (praise).

If tongues are used in public worship (as in 1 Corinthians 14) interpretation must be given (1 Corinthians 14:28). This is the special facility which the Spirit of God gives to some members of the body of Christ to make known to the other members of the body what has been uttered in an unknown tongue. James Packer in a recent book gives some examples which cast doubt on the authenticity of some interpretations of tongues.[28] Like prophecies, interpretations should be checked. In some cases, the leadership of the church could seek two independent interpretations of what is spoken in a tongue. We may make the following points.

1 The interpretation is not usually a translation of a human language. In that case a translation talent only would be required. This is a spiritual gift which reveals the essence of what has normally been uttered in a non-human language.

2 Several authorities claim that the gift-mix of speaking in tongues-interpretation of tongues is prevalent, i.e. a person who speaks in tongues in the congregation will often have the gift of interpretation. Paul appears to suggest in 1 Corinthians 14:13 that this is the usual pattern.[29]

One of the theses of this book is that our special gifts can be relied on so that we can plan our training and choose our long-term ministries in the light of ongoing gifts. This verse may appear to suggest that we may (or should) pray for additional gifts to those we already have. In response we may say that although there is a consistency and reliability in the Spirit's work in our lives there is also a sovereign freedom.

We may, and should, pray for gifts that will build up the body.

1 Markus Barth, *Ephesians* Translation and Commentary, Doubleday, N.Y. 1974, pp. 436 and 483 f.
2 *Baptism and Fullness*, Inter Varsity Press, London, 1964, p. 100.
3 *Ephesians* Vol 1, p.316.
4 C. Peter Wagner, *Your Spiritual Gifts Can Help Your Church Grow*, Regal, Glendale, 1979, p. 208.
5 Donald Bridge and David Phypers, *Spiritual Gifts and the Church*, Inter Varsity Press, London, 1973, p.36.
6 Bridge and Phypers, 1973, p.37.
7 Arnold Bittlinger, *Gifts and Ministries*, Hodder and Stoughton, London, 1974, p.93.
8 David Hill, *New Testament Prophecy*, John Knox Press, Atlanta, 1979, pp. 131-139.
9 The person with this gift of 'the word of knowledge' (1 Corinthians 12:8) always has a compulsion to share his or her knowledge. He or she may not, however, have the ability of the teacher in sharing simply and with clarity and order.
10 I see preaching as a learned art (and not a gift) which can take into its service a whole range of spiritual gifts.
11 A. Kittel (ed.), *Theological Dictionary of the New Testament*, Eerdmans, Grand Rapids, 1964, Vol VI, p. 498. See also Colin Brown (ed.), *Dictionary of New Testament Theology*, Paternoster, Exeter, 1978, Vol III, p. 568.
12 See the very helpful section in Wagner, pp. 142-153.
13 Note again that exhortation is distinguished from rebuke. Note also that the writer's exhortation is again related to the gospel: 'I charge you in the presence of God and of Christ Jesus . . . exhort' (2 Timothy 4:1-2).
14 Michael Green, *I Believe in the Holy Spirit*, Eerdmans, Grand Rapids, 1975, pp. 185-188.
15 The following treatment of the Old Testament material is based on that of Dr E. Schultz, Colin Brown (ed.) *Dictionary of New Testament Theology*, Paternoster, Exeter, 1978, Vol II, pp. 395 f.
16 Green, p. 184.
17 Wagner, pp. 218-20, 231.
18 Wagner, p. 103 f.
19 Green, p. 188.
20 In the *Didache*, an early Christian document, there is helpful advice concerning the discernment of the false prophet. A person who overstays his or her welcome or who sponges on others cannot be a true prophet. See Green, pp. 190-191.
21 These are those who have not yet heard the gospel in meaningful ways.
22 Wagner, pp. 213 f.
23 In his book on spiritual gifts Dr Wagner refers to this passage as supporting the existence of a charisma of martyrdom (p. 67).
24 Bridge and Phypers, p. 81.
25 *Theological Dictionary of the New Testament*, Vol IV, p. 507.
26 F. D. Bruner, *A Theology of the Holy Spirit*, Hodder and Stoughton, London, 1970, p. 192.
27 Peter Wagner does not think that there is a general gift which corresponds to the special gift of tongues. See *Your Spiritual Gifts Can Help Your Church Grow*, p. 235. Perhaps Romans 8:26 refers to the general gift. The argument against this latter view is that the main function for tongues is praise. Romans 8:26 refers to intercession. Of course there are other Christians who are not filled with the Spirit. Some of these may also speak in tongues (genuine or counterfeit). Love, including boldness to witness, and not speaking in tongues is the authentic sign of the Spirit's filling.

28 J. I. Packer, *Keep In Step With The Spirit*, Inter Varsity Press, Leicester, 1984, p. 212.
29 Green, p. 167 and Wagner, p. 235.

5

Serving gifts

As we have seen, the primary gifts of the risen Christ to his church are certain speaking or proclamation gifts including apostle, prophet, evangelist, pastor and teacher. The church lives by the Word of God (Matthew 4:4). The communication of the gospel is basic to its foundation and growth. Always some of the speaking gifts are listed first and given priority. (See 1 Peter 4:11, Ephesians 4:11, Romans 12:6-7, 1 Corinthians 12:8-10 and especially 12:28-31 and 14:1.)

Serving gifts, however, are also of enormous importance. In Romans 12 for example there is a strong emphasis on serving gifts.

These serving gifts come from Christ himself. He is *the* servant — fulfilling Old Testament prophecies concerning the suffering servant: the one who lays down his life as servant- Lord. Having their origin in him these servant gifts reflect him. The speaking gifts proclaim the gospel of the suffering servant. One function of the serving gifts is to authenticate the message delivered by the speaking gifts. In Hebrew thought the Word is never mere speech but speech plus deed. The speaking gifts plus the serving gifts together communicate the gospel of the Word made flesh. The deed makes the Word believable. Without them, the world remains unconvinced and unmoved.

In the serving gifts, word becomes deed. The gospel message about the suffering servant is lived out.

Without the serving gifts, the speaking gifts are unconvincing. The speaking gifts, however, must always have a certain priority in the church. Otherwise Christendom tends to lapse into religious humanism.

Gift 14
Service
Romans 12:7

To be a servant is to follow in the footsteps of the Lord who came 'not to be served but to serve, (from *diakoneo* which is related to *diakonia* service) and to give his life as a ransom for many' (Mark 10:45). Thus, whoever of Jesus' servants would be great must be the servant of his or her companions (verse 44).

All Christians must be servants — pouring out their lives for others. Every Christian must seek this gift and exercise it. Although every Christian must seek to exercise a general gift of service, there are those to whom the sovereign Spirit gives a special gift of service. The service of others — especially in practical ways — is their primary ministry. They are catalysts in the church for the ministry of service. They inspire and lead the church into new avenues of practical service. They are a conscience to the church, in the forefront of initiatives on behalf of the poor, the needy and victims of injustice.

Biblical teaching on service

Although many modern scholars warn against finding the origin for the office of deacon in Acts 6:1-6 it does seem reasonable to assume that the seven listed there had this gift of service.

In this passage Luke does not describe the seven as deacons (diakonoi). He does, however, use the word *diakonia* in verse 1 (daily distribution or service) and in verse 4 (ministry, or service, of the word) and *diakonein* (to serve) in verse 2 (serve tables). Only verse 2, of course, refers to what the seven did when they were appointed; they 'served tables'. Actually, they were given a fairly complex task which amounted to ensuring that the Greek widows were not disadvantaged — and that they received equal financial support with the Hebrew women.

The Greek word here for service or ministry (diakonia) occurs thirty-four times in the New Testament. It can have a wide range of meaning, but generally reflects a loving, caring attitude to those in need.

The serving church

We have seen that to be a servant is to follow in the footsteps of the servant Christ. It is to reflect the very essence of Christian faith. The church is thus called upon to be the servant church.

It is important to note that the special gift of service (which only some members of Christ's body have) may, like most other spiritual gifts, be exercised formally or informally, i.e. those with this gift may be appointed to a special office in the church which will allow them to concentrate on their gift — or they may exercise the gift informally and in unstructured ways.

It is no doubt important, wherever possible, to provide some opportunity for the formal exercise of this gift (as for other gifts like teaching, pastoring, evangelism, administration etc.). One way of doing this is by creating an office or order of deacon. We note, however, that those with this gift need not wait for such an office to be created — they may exercise their gifts informally in a whole variety of spontaneous ways. Further, when this order is established (see the *Basis of Union*, Uniting Church in Australia, paragraph 14 c) the function of this gift must not be restricted to the order. There are, no doubt, many people in an average congregation who have this special gift, and for whom there will never be a special office. They will have daily opportunities to exercise the gift.

The establishment of the Ministry of Deacon however, may have the following advantages:

1 It may assist in the identification of those scattered throughout the wider church who have a large gift of service.

2 It will give opportunity to those who are gifted and called to a serving ministry to be trained for ministry in our complex needy church and society. One of the emphases of this book is on the developing of gifts through training.

   Appointment to office depends not only on giftedness but also on training.

3 An order of deacon will provide opportunity for those with large serving gifts to concentrate on their gift. They will be paid for their services and their long term financial needs will be guaranteed. They will be able to give themselves to their ministry, without distraction.

4 The establishment of the diaconate will allow the Ministers of the Word to concentrate on the Ministry of the Word and on the gifts which the Spirit has given to them (Acts 6:4).

71

5 Full-time deacons will be catalysts for all in the congregation who have a special serving gift and for all others who have a general gift in this area. Such parish staff members will inspire and lead the whole parish into a variety of important serving ministries.

Since writing this material the Uniting Church Assembly has met and decided to establish a renewed Diaconate known as the Ministry of Deacon. The two-fold ministry of Word and Deacon appears to reflect in a very concrete way the two-fold emphasis of the New Testament teaching on gifts of speaking and gifts of serving. Both types of ministries are representative — they reflect the speaking and serving gifts which are spread throughout the whole church.

The church in Australia is called to serve our nation and the other nations of the world first of all by proclaiming the gospel of the servant Christ. Along with this proclamation the church must serve its members and its neighbours wherever it can, especially the suffering, the disadvantaged and victims of injustice. Some of those for whom the church in Australia has special responsibility are: the ill (especially those who are long-term or terminally ill), the lonely and depressed, the poor and socially disadvantaged (especially Aborigines, unemployed and refugees), the aged, and those who are often rejected by society on moral grounds (for example prisoners, homosexuals and prostitutes). The church's concern must extend, however, not only to these matters of social concern. It must also be concerned for social justice, (including efforts for peace, especially nuclear disarmament), human rights and the removal of oppression. The special gift of service which some Christians have may well be a catalyst for inspiring the whole church to give itself to service for Christ in the needy world which he came to serve and for which he died.

Questions Do you think it important for your denomination to establish a Diaconate? (If you are part of the Uniting Church, someone could give a summary of material from the Minutes of the Fourth Assembly, pages 11, 73-84.)

If so, what form should it take?

In the light of 1 Timothy 3:8-13 what qualities would you say are important for those who exercise (either formally or informally) the gift of service in our day?

Task List some of the specific concerns which the serving church in Australia might have.

Gift 15
Mercy
Romans 12:8

In the list of gifts in Romans 12 mercy (verse 8) is distinguished from service (verse 7). Not that we should think of the varying gifts as being entirely separate from one another. No doubt there is often a good deal of overlapping. Further, each gift takes many varying forms. It is probably true, for example, that every special gift of mercy will be different, to some extent, from every other gift of mercy. This is due mainly to the dynamic sovereignty of the Spirit but also due to the resulting individuality of personality, varying gift-mix, and so on.

It appears, however, that the gift of mercy is essentially person centred, whereas the gift of service may be task centred. The seven in Acts 6 have a task to perform. It is true that this task is essentially a work of compassion. It assists particular individuals. It is motivated by the love of Christ, but it is more task oriented than, say, the service of mercy of the Good Samaritan.

When I was serving as a minister in a church in North Hollywood, California, it was my task to do a good deal of visiting of the sick. It was amazing how often in my visits I would meet two of the dedicated ladies of the church, Effie and Margaret. They were often there before me and have regularly, as health has permitted, visited the shut-ins and those in special need. They, no doubt, have the gift of mercy. How necessary it is for this gift to be exercised if the proclamation of the gospel is to be backed up by loving deed.

One of the characteristics of this gift is cheerfulness. Many of us become depressed in the presence of suffering. Those with a gift of mercy have the God-given capacity to identify with those who are suffering and to remain cheerful. Effie, my good friend at North Hollywood, has this capacity. Over many years she herself suffered from the extremely painful complaint of tic douloureux. She was enabled not only to endure this pain but also to identify with others who were ill or lonely and to bring to them a great deal of genuine cheer.

The parable of the Good Samaritan teaches the need for all Christians to show compassionate mercy toward those in need. In contrast to the priest and Levite the Samaritan 'had compassion, and went to him and bound up his wounds' (Luke 10:33-34). Every Christian must show mercy when he or she finds a brother or sister by the roadside. Perhaps we shall not be far from understanding a special gift of mercy when we think of the person with this gift as having an amazing capacity not simply of helping the person whom he or she stumbles on by the wayside but of discovering that person well off the road. Such people have a capacity for discovering the needy and in compassion rallying the church to assist in alleviating that need.

Romans 12:8 emphasises that this gift should be exercised with cheerfulness. Those who work amongst the mentally or chronically ill or amongst the destitute (for example Mother Teresa in Calcutta) may easily be overcome by despair or discouragement. Only the Christian who lives by faith in a sovereign loving Father and by hope in a living, conquering, caring Christ can maintain a sense of cheerfulness in the face of hideous evil.

Despite the fact that those who have this gift are deeply moved with compassion toward the needy they are not overcome by sorrow. They identify with human need but retain a certain healthy objectivity. For them God never abdicates the throne of heaven. Genuine cheerfulness is always possible even as they 'weep with those who weep'. There is nothing superficial about this cheerfulness. It is an aspect of life-style. Despite the underlying seriousness of these Christians' outlook on life there is also a cheerfulness which in the end is catching.

This cheerfulness is totally unlike the attitude of many who visit the sick who perhaps cannot talk about the person's illness at all and simply indulge in superficial conversation — or who superficially pass the illness off with, 'You'll be right mate', or even, 'The Lord will heal you'. Mercy begins with compassion — with identifying with those who suffer. It weeps and suffers with the needy. But it does not leave the person in despair or sadness. Along with this compassion, empathy, weeping, and identification is also a genuine deep joy which is infectious. The person who has a special gift of mercy and who visits the sick, has a communicable disease: cheerfulness!

We may conclude then, that the gift of mercy is the special facility that some members of the body have in extraordinary measure (but which all members possess to some extent) of cheerfully reflecting the compassionate mercy of Christ in deeds which ease suffering.

The church's first responsibility is to its members (Galatians 6:10). This by no means implies that this work will be limited to members. It must include not only my brother and sister Christian but also my needy neighbour (Luke 10:33).

Those with a gift of mercy will be Christ's instruments of relieving human need and of motivating the church to action. They will be catalysts of mercy.

Gift 16a
Helping
1 Corinthians 12:28

Helps

Dr Raymond Ortlund, the pastor of the Lake Avenue Congregational Church, Pasadena, California, once described the people with this gift as the 'glorious company of the stretcher- bearers'. The reference, of course, is those who helped the man through the roof (Mark 2:1-12).[1] This gift is often unexciting and not as spectacular as speaking or miraculous gifts or even as some other serving gifts like leadership.

No doubt there are many people in an average congregation with this gift. If this gift is to be distinguished from mercy then the focus will be on the practical help which is given. Perhaps those with this gift are not capable of great amounts of empathy (like those with the gift of mercy) but they come to the aid of the weak (sick, poor, lonely, bereaved, aged, outcast) in all kinds of practical ways.

Our next door neighbour is a Christian. A few days after we moved into our present home there was a severe hail storm while we were out. The guttering of the house which was half full of leaves soon filled with hail stones, overflowed and flooded the basement of the house. In no time our neighbour was in to assist, clambouring around the high roof emptying out the guttering around the entire house. Peter appears to be the kind of person who never intrudes but who is eager to help in any situation. I would not be a bit surprised to find out that he has a special gift of helping.

Joe, his wife Con and daughter Julie also visited us soon after we moved house. They brought a number of beautiful trees and shrubs and spent a day and a half forming a new garden for us. Joe, as usual, brought his tools with him. He is one of the most helpful handymen I have ever met.

When we lived in the Port Kembla parsonage he and Albert, another member of the church, were on hand at any time of the day or night to do odd jobs. Now that both are retired I'm sure that a great deal of their daily life is spent in doing helpful things for the church and for needy people.

The important point to note about people like Joe and Albert is their dedication to Christ. All of this helping is done out of commitment to the Lord. Joe was converted during the Joe Blinco crusade in 1961. He has been witnessing ever since — in word and by helping people. He and his wife have participated in a Home Bible Fellowship since 1961 and they have a prayer meeting in their home on Monday mornings.

This helping gift can take many forms and it seems that in the average congregation there are many people with this gift. It is brought to life through the preaching of the gospel and it thrives in those congregations where a loving spirit prevails.

Biblical material

Helping or helps is mentioned as a gift in 1 Corinthians 12:28. The Greek word is *antilempsis*, literally meaning 'a laying hold of' (often with an aim of helping). Here it means the ministry of assistance. In the Greek version of the Old Testament the verbal form of this word often means 'to lay hold of' either literally or figuratively. We find it in the verse: 'Thou dost keep him in perfect peace, whose mind is stayed on thee' (Isaiah 26:3). The idea of help, however, is predominant in the Old Testament. It is used of helping one's neighbour some fourteen times and in reference to God some twenty times.

In Acts 20:35 Paul says to the Ephesian elders, 'In all things I have shown you that by toiling one must help (*antilambanesthai*) the weak, remembering the words of the Lord Jesus, how he said, "It is more blessed to give than to receive"'. Here Paul is stressing the need to help the sick. By working, he and those whom he is addressing not only cease to be a burden on others but they can actually help the sick who are unable to earn a living for themselves.

The Greek word *antilempsis* in 1 Corinthians 12:28 simply means 'help'. It is perhaps distinguished from the preceding gifts in that it is not generally miraculous. It may have a certain priority over the more spectacular gifts (administration and tongues) which follow.[2]

How do we differentiate between helping and showing mercy? Perhaps we should not make a hard and fast separation. No doubt 'mercy' emphasises the (cheerful) compassion and empathy which the servant of Christ shows to those in need, whereas helping refers to the support and aid which is given.

In the last analysis it is difficult to distinguish between mercy and helps. It may be that in reality they are the same gift. I can think of many people, however, who have a helping gift but who do not appear to have a gift of mercy — and vice versa. Few, I think, are those who have a special capacity for empathy. Those with the gift of helping, however, are doers. Certainly they are motivated by the gospel and by the love of Christ. But they are essentially practical people. My guess is that there are many more in the average church with this gift than with the gift of mercy.

Gift 16b
Assistance

Jan is a widow. She lives near her church. She cleans the church and loves to do it. She assists in all kinds of ways behind the scenes. She runs errands for the minister and is active in a thousand and one ways behind the scenes. Continuously she is assisting others so that they are released to do their own work and to concentrate on their gifts.

Jan is no leader. She never pushes herself on or takes over. She is essentially an assistant and a follower — a behind the scenes person. She is content with her gift. She is not jealous of those who have more spectacular gifts — who are up front people. Her gift is of great significance because she assists many people to exercise their gifts.

Other people with this gift might be stewards, care-takers, odd-job people — in fact, all who work behind the scenes and who help to free other people to exercise their gifts. Tentatively I add this gift to those listed in Scripture and call it the gift of assistance. I include it as a form of the helping gift.

Without making artificial or arbitrary distinctions between the four service gifts so far mentioned we may say that while all assist others in one way or another, I suggest that:

Service is task centred.

Mercy, helps and assistance are person to person ministries.

Mercy is characterised by empathy and compassion which motivates the person with the gift.

Helps focuses on aid actually given to the weak.

Assistance focuses on help given to the strong (to release them to exercise their gifts).

As with all the serving gifts meekness is needed if this gift is to be exercised fully to the glory of God. Servanthood requires humility.

The gift of assistance especially requires meekness. Those who have this gift need grace which permits them to take second place, to avoid the limelight, to push others on. Those with a poor self-image who find it necessary to put others down and to elevate themselves will easily misuse this gift. Those with this gift often need encouragement.

Questions Do you think that there is such a special gift as assistance? If not, why not?

If so, can you think of a better name?

Do the following passages contain examples of those who might have this gift?

1 Peter 5:12; Exodus 18:21-22; Numbers 11:16-17; Romans 16:1-2; 1 Timothy 6:2

Gift 17
Voluntary poverty
1 Corinthians 13:3

Voluntary poverty seems to be a Spirit-given ability to develop a very simple lifestyle and to be content with it — so that one can serve others in concentrated effort and with a generous spirit.

Is not every Christian called to live in simplicity (if not poverty) for the sake of the gospel and the sake of others? Yes. And there are many prophets in our day who are calling the affluent members of the western church to simplicity and generosity for the sake of the lost and the poor.

I wish to endorse that call. I think that it is possible that one means by which the Spirit of God is calling the whole church to simplicity and generosity for the sake of the needy in its ranks and the world beyond its doors is through the gift of voluntary poverty. Those with this gift can be an inspiration to the church and through their identification with the poor and by their generous giving a source of relief to the needy. They can also be agents of the gospel. Sometimes the gift seems to be combined with prophecy. In that case a powerful prophetic call to simplicity is backed up by a lifestyle where poverty is incarnated.

The biblical material on voluntary poverty

There is not a great deal of direct biblical support for the existence of a special gift of voluntary poverty. 1 Corinthians 13:3 says 'If I give away all I have, and if I deliver my body to be burned, but have not love, I gain nothing'. The first part of this verse is thought by some experts on spiritual gifts to refer to a special gift of voluntary poverty.[3]

It seems best, however, to conclude that although Paul may be referring to a special gift of voluntary poverty in 1 Corinthians 13:3, he is more likely to be referring to the gift of giving (or mercy) exercised to the utmost degree. It is, however, just possible that this is a special kind of gift of giving — one that runs itself into poverty. The emphasis even here, however, (when the gift is properly exercised) should be on the loving giving of one's goods (to the poor) and not on the poverty of the giver.

Examples of voluntary poverty

Scripture does not necessarily contain an exhaustive list of gifts. A study of church history may supplement the biblical list.

John Wesley appears to have had this gift. He probably could have become a very rich man through his extensive publications. He claimed that he never spent more than thirty pounds per year on himself. Any surplus he had was given to the poor or towards the expenses of the Revival. He wore neatly mended shirts, never wore a wig and frequently cut his own hair to save the price of a barber. On one occasion he wrote to the tax collector in London saying that he had two silver spoons, one in London and one in Bristol and that he would never have more while men around him still wanted bread.[4] He distributed thirty thousand pounds during his lifetime.[5]

Other examples of voluntary poverty appear to be St. Francis of Assisi of the 12th-13th century and Mother Teresa of Calcutta in our own day — and multitudes of others like them who, not because of a blanket requirement to live in poverty but because of a special gift, have served their Lord, the gospel and the poor in freedom through poverty. The evangelical members of Sojourners and other Christian communities are probably other examples. C. T. Studd appears to have had this gift.[6]

Simplicity and voluntary poverty

Throughout this book I have stressed the importance of general gifts (or Christian roles) and special gifts, arguing that there appears to be a general gift, which every Christian may have in increasing measure, and a special gift which only some Christians have. I suggest that the general gift which corresponds to the special gift of voluntary poverty is simplicity. This general gift which is emphasised strongly in Scripture, appears to be of enormous importance in an affluent but needy world and could be one of particular importance to the Uniting Church in Australia.

Those with the gift of voluntary poverty may provide leadership for the whole church in terms of service. They may be catalysts for the work amongst the poor. Perhaps one of their most important functions is the stimulation of the wider general gift of simplicity.

There are several New Testament persons who were called to poverty, either temporarily or permanently. Some may have had this gift. For our sakes, our Lord became poor (2 Corinthians 8:9), he left behind (apparently) only a seamless coat (John 19:23) — no doubt the gift of a loving friend. Simon and Andrew left their livelihood to follow Jesus (Mark 1:18). John and James did the same (verse 20). The rich young ruler was called to poverty and to follow Jesus (Mark 10:21). It would, no doubt be incorrect to read into this passage a reference to a special gift of poverty. No doubt there are, however, many who are offered a gift of poverty by the risen Christ but who go away sorrowful — unable to receive such a wonderful gift of grace. Zacchaeus spontaneously offered to give one half of his goods to the poor and Barnabas willingly brought his money and laid it at the apostles' feet.

The common practice, however, of selling one's property in order to share with the other members of the church soon ceased.[7] Perhaps this practice overlooked the fact that not every Christian has the spiritual gift of poverty. Ananias and Sapphira were probably not the only ones who found it difficult to give their all.

Voluntary poverty has various motives and uses. In the early church the motive was the meeting of human need (Acts 2:45, 4:34-35). Some have given away their wealth because they have felt too attached to it. It seems that this was behind our Lord's calling to the rich young ruler (Mark 10:21). Others find a freedom and lack of distraction in their service through this gift. Some, no doubt, are able to release considerable resources for missionary work in this way. Some find it a way of identifying with the poor; others (like George Muller) of proving God's faithfulness. Others, no doubt, find it a helpful first step in developing a life of simplicity.

Conclusion

Whatever we may call simplicity, we are all called upon to adopt it as a lifestyle which reflects an inner grace. Whatever we may call voluntary poverty some are called to exercise it for the sake of Christ and his kingdom.

Questions Since voluntary poverty may be best exercised in a community, should the Uniting Church in Australia, and other denominations, encourage the establishment of Christian communes?

Could there be a place within the ordained ministry for a special order for those who have the gift of voluntary poverty and who can find mutual support in a ministry to the poorer areas and communities of our land and overseas?

Gift 18
Giving
Romans 12:8

Doug and Judith are two of the most generous people I have met. They were wonderfully converted during the 1959 Billy Graham Crusade. Since then their whole lifestyle has radiated generosity. Doug is a chemist and pharmacist. Soon after their conversion Doug and Judith took time off to go to Bible College. They took their four children with them — so the expense was great. When we first met them they were prominent in the parish which we were serving. The income from the larger of their two pharmacies was entirely given to the Lord's work. Many people in different parts of the world benefitted.

Doug had a vision for a long time concerning a Christian camp site. About 1971 he sold his home and one pharmacy and bought a large property on the south coast of New South Wales. He has handed over the property to a trust and now manages the camp site. From the lovely home which he has built near the camp site he still exercises his gift of giving and with Judith combines it with generous hospitality.

The greatest thing about the gifts which Doug and Judith exercise is the motive. It is always the love of Christ which inspires them. Their giving and their hospitality are without ulterior motive. One always feels at home with them — relaxed and welcome. Their love and generosity reflect that of the Father who gives to the just and unjust and who gives generously — with 'good measure, pressed down, shaken together, running over' (Luke 6:38). It has been one of the great privileges of my life to have known Doug and Judith and to have had them as friends. I know God a little better through them. Their lifestyle reflects something of the generosity of the Father of abundant grace.

Biblical concept of giving

This gift is referred to in Romans 12:8. It is the Greek word *metadidous* from *meta* 'with' and *didomi* 'to give' and means giving a share. Most commentators think that this refers to giving away what is one's own , although Calvin may be correct when he interprets it as referring to distribution of church funds.

Paul says earlier in this same letter, 'For I long to see you that I may impart (*metado*) to you some spiritual gift to strengthen you' (Romans 1:11). In Ephesians 4:28 Paul says, 'Let the thief no longer steal, but rather let him labour, doing honest work with his hands, so that he may be able to give (share — *metadidonae*) to those in need'.

John the Baptist urged those who were truly repentant: 'He who has two coats, let him share (*metadoto*) with him who has none; and he who has food, let him do likewise' (Luke 3:11). In 1 Thessalonians 2:8 Paul writes, 'So, being affectionately desirous of you, we were ready to share (*metadounai*) with you not only the gospel of God but also our own selves (literally souls), because you had become very dear to us'.

The gift of giving, then, is the gift of sharing. We assume that in Romans 12:8 it refers to the special ability that some Christians have to share their material possessions with others.

Those who share with others must do it 'in liberality'. The Greek word is *haplotes* which means either sincerity (from *haplous*, single, simple, in contrast to *diplous*, double), or liberality. If we take the first meaning the emphasis will be a giving without ulterior motive, such as winning influence or, pandering to pride and self-satisfaction. In the context of Romans 12 this refers back to those who are justified by faith (chapters 1-4) who are in union with the crucified and risen Christ (chapter 5), who are being led by the Spirit (chapter 8), and who are being renewed in mind. Their motives are pure, therefore their giving is single minded.

The gift of giving is the special facility which the risen Christ has given through his Spirit to some members of the Body in extraordinary measure (but to all Christians in some increasing? measure) to share, in response to the gospel, their money and other possessions with generosity and especially without ulterior motives.

All Christians are called upon to give generously out of a response to the generous giving of our great God. Paul writes to the Corinthians, 'You will be enriched in every way for great generosity . . . Under the test of this service, you will glorify God by your obedience in acknowledging the gospel of Christ, and by the generosity of your contribution for them and for all others' (2 Corinthians 9:11-13). The gospel prompts a generous spirit in every genuine Christian. There are, nevertheless, those Christians who have a special capacity to give. It is important to note that a person does not have to be rich to have the gift of giving. The widow who gives her two mites may have this gift.

Although those with the gift of giving are to give as anonymously as possible (Matthew 6:3) so that the motive for their giving will not be compromised, their generous lifestyles will nevertheless inspire others to give. They will naturally teach others to give in more formal ways and draw attention of the church to needy causes.

No doubt the Australian and other western churches need to learn to give generously. Under the law, Jews were required to give a tithe, or a tenth. Actually in special and free will offerings they gave much more than a strict tithe. In many Christian churches, tithing is taught and practised. It seems to me, however, that under grace the strict teaching of tithing is contrary to the gospel. It is a return to legalism. Tithing can be both too harsh and too easy. For some whose poverty is great, who incurred great debts before becoming Christians, who have large families or who are in chronic ill-health, a strict tenth may be a level of giving which they find beyond their willingness or ability to give (2 Corinthians 8:12; Acts 11:29). They should not be brought into bondage by the teaching of strict tithing.

For most in the affluent western world a tenth is too easy. Many Christians with a simplified lifestyle may be able to give 20% or 50% or more. A legalistic teaching of tithing may fail to lift the sights of men and women of faith so that they can see the true potential to give as heirs of grace.

For many Christians the tithe may be a convenient point to begin — provided this standard is not understood in any legalistic way.[8] We may well reason 'If the Jew under law gave more than a tenth, can I under grace give any less?'

Gratitude can never be satisfied with a tithe if it has the resources to give more. It will realise that if a person can give a tenth on $15,000 a year, he or she can give more than a tenth if the salary is suddenly increased to $20,000. If a person can give one tenth while paying off the house, he or she can probably give much more when the payments are complete.

Some Christians speak about a 'graduated tithe' — the more you make, the larger the percentage (not just the amount) you give. Perhaps Christians should set goals for themselves — that in a certain period of time (when they are able to simplify their lifestyle — buy a smaller house, sell one of their cars and some of their excess belongings) they will consider raising their giving by 5 or 10 or 20%. As we give a certain amount we learn to give and so are able to give more and trust God more to provide for our needs.

As we observe those who have a gift of giving, let us not feel guilty so much as inspired. Let us not give what others give, but what we can willingly and freely give by the power of God's spirit.

Questions What do you think of the concept of graduated tithe? What safeguards are needed?

How do you respond to Wesley's advice, 'Gain all you can, save all you can, give all you can'?

Describe the special gift of giving. How can this gift be used in evangelism and caring?

Gift 19
Leadership
Romans 12:8

Spiritual gifts and leadership in the church

We have progressed beyond the concept of the church as a one person bus. But do we go to the other extreme with every passenger endeavouring to drive the bus? Thus we have a picture of a rather large bus containing fifty bus drivers all snatching at the steering wheel. Few, if any has bothered to gain a licence — anyone can drive a bus! The original driver has been ousted from the driver's seat and sits by him or herself at the back of the bus.

Meanwhile with all the pulling and shoving, not to speak of the commotion, the bus has not even been started. If it does eventually get going what direction will it take? Everyone has a different notion concerning the best route — everyone does what is wise in his or her own eyes.

So the one person bus is in danger of being replaced by the every person bus. There is now no driver since everyone is driving. If everyone leads nobody leads. If everyone leads nobody follows.

Spiritual gifts and church order

We turn to 1 Timothy 4:14: 'Do not neglect the gift you have, which was given you by prophetic utterance when the elders laid their hands upon you.' What is the gift which Timothy received?

There are essentially three interpretations:

It refers to the *office* Timothy was given — the oversight of several churches.

It refers to general *spiritual grace* to enable him to fulfil his ministry.

It refers to *specific spiritual gifts* (like leadership, teaching, pastoring and evangelism).

The context makes it clear that Timothy had a certain leadership and teaching authority in the church. It may be unwise to define Timothy's gift too narrowly but to see it as a reference to his overall gift-mix or to the grace which he received to fulfil his office as a leader-teacher in the church of God.

This passage of Scripture seems to have implications for us today.

1 If we are to carry out any special ministry for Christ we will need grace. And God never commissions anyone to a task without the Spirit giving him or her the grace-gifts to fulfil it.

2 This gift came to Timothy through the elders (i.e. through the church). We have seen throughout that gifts-teaching in the New Testament is always presented in the context of the church. There is a false spirituality which so emphasises the individual's call and his or her relationship to God that the church as God's instrument is neglected. Spiritual gifts are not a private affair. They relate to the church. They are not inconsistent with church order, ordination or eldership.

3 Church order and the freedom of the Spirit are not necessarily mutually exclusive. Timothy's gift is here associated with both charismatic prophecy and ordination. Not order or ardour. Both.

4 The text is a command to every Christian, 'Do not neglect the gift that you have', or as 2 Timothy 1:6 puts it, 'rekindle the gift of God that is within you'. Do not let the fire die. We keep and develop our gifts as we give ourselves to our ministry. Exercise strengthens. Neglect atrophies.

I find it encouraging to think that Christ chose Timothy, of all people, to exercise leadership in his church — poor, weak, timid Timothy. He was a super-sensitive person who was reluctant to exercise his gifts with power. His upset stomach and frequent ailments could easily have been a function of his nervous temperament.

In leadership he was probably indecisive, hesitant and defensive. In evangelism, teaching and exhortation he may have been reluctant (partly because of his comparative youth) to preach, teach and exhort with boldness and authority. Spiritual gifts theology which releases the whole membership for ministry is one sided unless it also emphasises leadership gifts.

After Timothy has been exhorted to rekindle his gift, the explanation is given: 'for God did not give us a spirit of timidity but a spirit of power and love and self-control'(2 Timothy 1:7). Again we see that gifts (leadership and teaching) without graces (power and self-control) are ineffective. Note that power without love and self-control is harsh and inadequate. Authority becomes authoritarianism. Nothing could be less needed in the church of Christ. Nothing could be more contrary to the spirit of Jesus who led by serving. Strong humble leadership is desperately needed in the church of God which releases its whole membership for ministry.

Hebrews 13:17 reads, 'Obey your leaders and submit to them; for they are keeping watch over your souls, as men who will have to give account. Let them do this joyfully, and not sadly, for that would be of no advantage to you'.

The obedience should not be blind nor should the authority be absolute. The leaders are also under authority — they have to give an account. The leading is never authoritarian. The leading and the following are both in love and both in meekness. But there must be leaders who serve those who follow and there must be followers who honour their leaders.

Gifts-theology releases a huge multitude for ministry. The multitude will be like sheep without a shepherd if it does not have strong leaders.

Normally the minister will be the leader of the leaders. That ought to be freely acknowledged. It should never have to be imposed. Since the minister is a Minister of the Word the power by which he or she leads resides essentially in that Word. It does not reside in him or her, but in Christ to whom the Word bears witness.

It seems, then, that the New Testament teaching on gifts does not in any way subtract from the importance of those whom we call 'Ministers of the Word'. Their function (with the elders) is two fold.

1 **In terms of ministry.** It is not to do all the ministry — that task is too vast. It is to equip the saints for ministry (Ephesians 4:11-12). The Uniting Church in Australia *Basis of Union* puts it clearly. They 'will preach the Gospel, administer the sacraments and exercise pastoral care so that all may be equipped for their particular ministries, thus maintaining the apostolic witness to Christ in the Church' (paragraph 14a).

2 **In terms of leadership.** They shall lead the congregation. They are called and commissioned to oversight. Ministers are

coaches in ministry and leaders in the 'government' of their church.

Leadership is a spiritual gift mentioned in Romans 12:8. It speaks of those who 'have authority'. It is the Greek word *prois-tamenos*. Pro means 'before' and *istamenos* means 'standing'. It means 'standing before' or 'taking the lead'. A possible model was the leader of the synagogue — the person who stood before the congregation and led the people. Prof. Reicke writing in Kittel's *Theological Dictionary of the New Testament* argues that caring was the responsibility of the leading members of the early church.[9] In Romans 12:8 this gift comes between sharing and showing kindness. The emphasis in leadership, he says, is not on rank or authority, but on pastoral care.

1 Thessalonians 5:12 has a similar thought, 'But we beseech you . . . to respect those who labour among you and are over you in the Lord' i.e. lead (*proistamenos*) and admonish (exhort) you.

After treating each New Testament occurrence of this word Prof. Reicke concludes that in all these instances the verb has in the New Testament the primary meaning of both to lead and to care for and that this agrees with the distinctive nature of office in the New Testament. It thus agrees with the spirit of Jesus when he says in Luke 22:25-26, 'The kings of the Gentiles exercise lordship over them. . . But not so with you; rather let the greatest among you become as the youngest, and the leader as one who serves'.

Leadership in the church in Australia

I have suggested that maximum quality and quantity church growth is likely to take place when most of the ministry is being done by the congregation (through the exercise of spiritual gifts) and when the key leadership role is given to the minister (as servant-leader and as leader of leaders). The church in Australia needs to allow its gifted leaders to lead. Normally this leader will be one of the ministers in the parish — who is gifted and trained in leadership, called by Christ and appointed by the church to lead the parish.

Ministers ought to be taught to lead. I have spent many years in formal study developing pastoral, teaching and knowledge gifts. Since my youth I have held many positions of leadership outside and inside the church and in para-church organisations. I think I have a certain gift of leadership — and have had much experience in leadership. I have, however, received no formal training in leadership. It seems a tragedy that in a day when so much expertise in leadership is available I was thrust out into responsible positions of parish leadership without adequate training. There appears to be an obvious on-going need to take into account spiritual gifts (including leadership) when drawing up the curriculum in our theological colleges.

Congregations need to learn to follow. The priesthood of all believers means that any and every Christian may discern the will of God for the whole congregation. This priesthood will be more effective when it meets together. This underlines the importance of the Congregational Meeting and of the need for leaders to be open to the views and contributions by members, including youth and children, of the congregation. The congregation has some part to play in the decision making process, but it must nevertheless be generally ready to honour the decisions of its God appointed leaders (Hebrews 13:17).[10]

Questions Does the church in Australia have weaknesses because of weak leadership?

The gifts of leadership do not seem to be lacking, but are they exercised with power and love and self-control? Do we simply leave the problems in our parishes and denominations to drift?

What needs to be done if the church of the future is to be assured of well-trained competent and godly leadership?

Gift 20
Faith
1 Corinthians 12:9

The Council of Elders looked like concluding by 9.30 pm. All the business had proceeded smoothly as usual. Indeed over the last couple of years the Council had settled down into a convenient comfortable rut! Just then Mary Smith rose to her feet and presented her vision for the parish. She saw clearly that God was leading the parish into a period of rapid growth through evangelism. It is possible that Mary here was exercising the special spiritual gift of faith.

Biblical teaching

Of course, every Christian has faith for without faith it is impossible to please God (Hebrews 11:6). We become Christians through faith (i.e. trust) in Christ and we live the Christian life by faith. Over and above this general gift of faith which every Christian has, however, there is a special gift of faith. In 1 Corinthians 12:9 we are told that some Christians are given the gift of faith by the Spirit. Before we examine this particular text we need to see what biblical faith generally means. In the New Testament faith (*pistis*) is dependent on grace (*charis*); see Ephesians 2:8. Grace is God's free favour which comes to us through Christ. Faith is dependence on this grace. As the Reformers reminded us, we are saved by grace through faith.

We may say that New Testament faith has the following qualities:

It abandons self-reliance and looks to the crucified and risen Christ alone for salvation.

Faith is concerned with facts (what God has done in Christ).

It is often followed by 'that' (John 8:24).

It is essentially trust in Christ. The verb 'to believe' is often followed by 'into' (eis). Faith brings us into a personal relationship with Christ.

93

Faith leads to love and obedience.

We are saved by grace alone through faith alone. Although we become Christians by an act of faith we need to continue in faith.

When we return to 1 Corinthians 12:9 and the special gift of faith we may say that although this gift is not to be identified with saving faith nor with the faith that every Christian continues to have, it must be understood in terms of general New Testament teaching on faith. It is centred in Christ and the gospel. It despairs of self. It is essentially trust. It results in obedience and love.

Since faith is centred in Christ this gift is not referring to a human quality of faith (thought of as independent of its object, Christ). It is not a matter of auto suggestion. It is not merely a matter of believing that something wonderful will happen. It is concerned with faith in Christ.

The gift of faith, then, is not different in kind from the faith which every Christian exercises. It is a difference in degree. Those with this special gift seem to have an extraordinary ability (by God's grace alone) to trust God. Perhaps we need to think of it as intensive faith. Although Mark 9:23 and Matthew 17:20 probably are intended to apply to every Christian, these verses may give us a glimpse of the kind of faith which those with this special gift regularly demonstrate (but which other Christians show to a lesser extent). To those with this gift 'mountain moving faith' is an outstanding, recurring feature of their lifestyle. This faith seems also to have an element of vision in it. Those with this gift seem to be able to see with extraordinary clarity what God can do through his people.

Church leadership and church growth

This gift appears to be of great significance for visionary leadership and church growth. Those with this gift are able to inspire the church to lift its vision concerning evangelistic and pastoral growth of the church. It is important in setting goals, planning, commencing new ministries and undertaking specific growth projects. Those with this gift (especially ministers, elders and other leaders) are possibility thinkers who are not deterred by difficulties, opposition (although they may be irritated by criticism) and suffering.[11] They are often the inspiration for new ministries. They seem to be able to see where God can lead the church over the next decade or so. They are generally optimistic.

For the church to realise its full potential in evangelistic growth this gift of faith, together with that of leadership, may be the two most important gifts which the ministerial leader can have.

The person who has this gift needs humility (lest he or she becomes proud) and patience with those who are not able quickly to see the specific vision. Humility is also needed to recognise that since, 'we see in a mirror dimly' (1 Corinthians 13:12), our best visions have their blind spots. Thus the person with this gift (who can tend to be impractical and over optimistic) needs to have around him or her a group of leaders with the gifts of wisdom (especially), administration, prophecy, knowledge etc., who can help to mould the vision so that it reflects more clearly the mind of God.

On the other hand, since such dreamers are often sensitive to criticism, they also need encouragement. The elders (especially) need to be open to the dreams and visions of ministers and others who have this gift. They do not need to endorse every dream, but they do need to be open to what the Spirit may be saying to the church through the person who has this gift.

The gift of faith is to be distinguished from the faith (or faithfulness) which is understood as fruit of the Spirit (Galatians 5:22).

This gift of serving faith, then, is the special facility which the Spirit of God gives to some Christians by which they are able to see (vision) with remarkable assurance strategies of ministry related to the purposes of God and to trust him until the vision is realised. It is accompanied by earnest, confident prayer (i.e. the prayer of faith). It is generally related to specific situations. It may involve dreaming specific plans for the kingdom of God and moving ahead with humble confidence to share and implement these plans for the sake of the body.

All of us need to exercise a general gift in this area. Let us encourage those who have a special gift of faith by being open to their dreams and by working to implement their visions according to the insights of the whole body.

Question Encourage someone to give a book review or give some details from the life of a Christian who appeared to have this gift (for example George Muller).

What are the characteristics of the special gift of faith?

Gift 21
Administration
1 Corinthians 12:28

Lilian is an elder in a country parish. She is also secretary of the Parish Council. She has an obvious administrative gift which is recognised throughout the parish. She does not impose her gift on the church, but exercises it in great humility. People constantly turn to her for direction in parish affairs. She works in conjunction with others.

Biblical material

In 1 Corinthians 12:28 Paul refers to 'administrators' as those who possess a special charisma in order to serve the church. The Greek word *kuberneseis* means literally 'helmsman'. (A form of this Greek word is used in Acts 27:11 to refer to the captain of a ship.) It may be translated here as 'gifts of direction' (or governing). Such a person steers or directs the congregation. The life of the early church was so fluid at this time that we do not really know the precise scope of this gift. We do know, however, that just as the importance of a captain (or pilot) in a ship increases during a storm so the importance of this gift increases during periods of stress in the life of the church.

This gift is basically a service gift rather than a speaking gift. The administrator does not necessarily preach. The apostles, prophets and teachers do not necessarily have this gift of directing the order and life of the local congregation. Because this word comes after the gifts of healing and helping and before tongues then it may relate to keeping order and mediating within the life of the church.[12] The need for such a function in the life of the church is seen in 1 Corinthians 14:40 — a verse which deals with tongues.

It has been suggested that helpers and administrators may have foreshadowed the work of local deacons and bishops (or elders)[13] respectively. The gift of administration, however, may no doubt be exercised informally (i.e. without appointment to office) although the scope for its exercise will no doubt be limited without official recognition.

It may be that this gift and tongues are placed at the end of Paul's list because there needed to be a corrective to the Corinthians' preference for self-assertive gifts.

It does not seem possible to describe from Scripture what this specific gift is. It may be associated with leadership (Romans 12:8) and with eldership. It may have been important for steering the troubled church through difficult times and for keeping order and peace within the body. Without this leadership-steering-oversight-mediating, other gifts may easily get out of hand and the body split.

Is it possible that today we have two forms of this gift?

1 Administrational leadership

It seems likely that administration in 1 Corinthians 12:28 is a leadership gift. It may be that we have here two gifts — a gift mix of administration and leadership. It appears more likely, however, that Paul has in mind that this person administers (steers) the local church by a certain kind of gift of leadership. Other people in the church may have a gift of leadership of a different kind. They inspire the church but do not necessarily steer (administer) it.

John Wesley and George Whitefield were the two key leaders of the evangelical awakening of the 18th century. Wesley led and administered (steered) this movement by directing converts into class meetings. Whitefield's work on the other hand has been described as a 'rope of sand'. He was an inspiring leader of the Revival but he did not administer it. He had no organisational or administrative gift. Although Wesley's form of the gift has an organisational aspect the essence of the gift appears to be in terms of leadership. An important aspect of Wesley's administrative gift was his ability to organise every aspect of the work of Methodism and to direct converts and adherents into class meetings. The more important aspect of his gift, however, was the authoritative leadership which he exercised.

There is a great ongoing need in the church in Australia for administrative leaders who have this charisma. The church needs to pray that God will raise up those who will exercise this gift in the power of God's Spirit. The church continues to need men and women who can steer the church through these difficult times.

2 Administrational organisation

This form of the gift appears to be closely related to what we may call a talent of administration. It refers to an organisational ability. It is the special facility that some Christians have of efficiently organising the body of Christ for worship, nurture, witness and service. In this form it is not necessarily a leadership gift and may not be what Paul had in mind in 1 Corinthians 12:28. For the modern church it seems to be a very important gift.

Parish life today is very complex. Large parishes with several centres and many varying ministries and activities, complex denominational structures, the complexity of modern life, the availability of a huge reservoir of administrative know-how and the church's access to advancing technology all demand thorough organisation. If the whole church is to be released for ministry and exercise all its varying gifts then without efficient organisation, parish life will soon be in disarray and ministers and other leaders will continue to be under great stress.

The church has tended to lag behind the rest of the community in its strategic and wise use of technology and administrative skills. Not that we should make our organisation over complex by completely copying modern business organisation. Wisely and prayerfully the church needs to become efficient in its administration at the parish level.

Elsewhere I have stressed the importance of growing churches establishing a parish office which is run by an administrative elder (parish co-ordinator) or secretary who works with and under the direction of office bearers.[14] There will be many opportunities for those with this kind of organisational administrative gift to serve in the church and para-church groups. Even when not appointed to office they will exercise their gift informally. This form of the gift of administration is of great importance in co-ordinating and releasing other members of the body to exercise their gifts and to co-ordinate the wide range of ministries in the modern complex parish.

One final word. It may be that one of the chief tasks of the administrator is to assist the church to simplify its life and organisation — to streamline it for efficient witness and nurture. In so doing the administrators may assist many Christians to be more relaxed and human in their daily lives.

Questions Do you think that there are two kinds of administrative gifts?

Can you name specific people who have administrative gifts? Perhaps your group would like to pray for them.

Gift 22
Celibacy
1 Corinthians 7:7

Betty was attracted to a young man when she was in her early twenties, but nothing came of the friendship. Later she felt the call of God to full-time service. In this service she has served Christ in unhindered ways. Her whole life is dedicated to his work. Sometimes she is lonely and wishes she had married, but mostly she is able to give herself to her work and to her Lord.

In 1 Corinthians 7:7 celibacy appears to be described as a spiritual gift (charisma). It is natural that we should interpret this use of charisma in terms of Paul's teaching in the remainder of this letter (for example 1:7; chapters 12-14). If this is so then celibacy (singleness) is a gift like others we have described.

In Matthew 19:12 Jesus says, 'For there are eunuchs who have been so from birth, and there are eunuchs who have been made eunuchs by men, and there are eunuchs who have made themselves eunuchs for the sake of the kingdom of heaven. He who is able to receive this, let him receive it'.

It was the unanimous teaching of the rabbis that the duty of every Israelite was to marry and have children. This was simply following the 'order of creation' as set out in Genesis 1:28 and 2:24. Eunuchs who were sexually defective and who could not follow this law were excluded from the community of Israel (Deuteronomy 23:1) although the prophet Isaiah looked forward to the day when the eunuch would be welcomed into the kingdom of God (56:3 f).

In Matthew 19:12 Jesus describes three kinds of eunuchs. In describing the first two types he is identifying with the teaching of the rabbis. His description of the third type of eunuch is new. The prophecy of Isaiah is fulfilled because with the coming of Jesus the kingdom has arrived. The kingdom takes precedence over creation (and the creation ordinance of marriage).

We should understand this third reference to eunuchs in a figurative spiritual sense. It is a reference to celibacy. In the first instance it may be a reference to Jesus himself. For the sake of the kingdom he remained celibate. (Perhaps the rabbis were criticising him for this.)

The church has not always come to terms with the biblical concept of singleness. Often it has shown an insensitivity to celibacy by over-emphasising the joys of nuclear family life, the importance of motherhood and child-bearing, and the normalcy of the married state. There is a resulting pressure on young singles to commit themselves to relationships which may not be healthy. This situation is complicated by the fact that in all of us (including those with the gift of celibacy) there is the struggle to cope with one's sexuality as well as the need to be special to someone. With the arrival of the kingdom in Jesus all (even the defective eunuch who cannot obey the creation ordinance) are welcome among God's people. For the sake of the kingdom some are called to singleness. Single persons are no longer excluded from the people of God; nor are they second class citizens of the kingdom; they are first class citizens along with their celibate Lord.

In Matthew 19:11 Jesus said to his disciples, 'Not all men can receive this precept, but only those to whom it is given'. The question is, what does Jesus mean by 'this precept'? Jesus had been reaffirming the permanence of marriage and speaking against easy divorce and redressing an imbalance against women. The disciples, on hearing this, felt that it would be better not to marry. Jesus then speaks in verse 11 (as above). 'This precept' does not refer to the saying of Jesus in verse 9, and probably not to the saying of the disciples in verse 10, but to the precept (Genesis 1:27, 2:24) quoted in verse 5.[15]

Jesus teaches that not everyone can receive the command to marry (Genesis 2:24) but only those to whom it is given. There are at least three kinds of persons who are excepted from obeying the command to marry — those who are sexually defective from birth, those who have been made such by man's inhumanity, and those who are celibate for the sake of the kingdom. Persons ought not to abstain from marriage for inadequate reason and certainly not (as the disciples had suggested in verse 10) simply because it appears difficult to sustain a life-long relationship with one person. Jesus concludes, 'He who is able to receive this, (i.e. the command to marry) let him receive it' (verse 12b).

If this interpretation is correct Jesus may be saying that all who are physically able to marry should normally marry unless they remain single (and celibate) for the sake of the kingdom of heaven. In 1 Corinthians 7:7 Paul says, 'I wish that all were as I myself am (i.e. single or able to resist sexual temptation). But each has his own special gift (charisma) from God, one of one kind and one of another'.

It seems clear that celibacy here is described as a special gift which only some Christians receive. Linking this passage with the Matthew 19 passage we can say that those who are given the gift (charisma) of celibacy make themselves eunuchs (figurative language for celibate) for the sake of the kingdom. In other words the special gift of celibacy received from the Spirit makes it permissible for these particular Christians not to receive the creation command which has been given to all others. Some scholars think that marriage also is a special gift.

We note the following characteristics and implications of the gift of singleness.

> Those with this gift are first class citizens in the kingdom of God. We should, therefore, not subject them to sly and hurtful remarks about those who are 'on the shelf'.

> Celibacy is a special calling (gift). Whereas it is not an inferior way of life (as some Protestants have implied) it is not a superior way of life (as some Catholics have implied).

> There are advantages in singleness, especially in times of upheaval (1 Corinthians 7:26). The single person is free from anxiety concerning caring for a partner and children and is able to give him or herself to the work of the Lord with less distraction. Such a person is usually able to give him or herself in devotion to the Lord. Such a gift can be of great importance for the growth of the church.

> Celibacy, then, is not a superior or inferior way of life. It does have certain advantages as far as serving the kingdom is concerned. The best lifestyle, however, as far as the individual is concerned is to accept the will of God for one's own life, whether that be marriage (according to God's general creation ordinance) or celibacy (if one has a special gift).

> Celibacy, and perhaps the missionary gift, are the two gifts which we may assume are never given on their own. Singleness allows a person to give maximum effort to the exercise of his or her other gifts.

> Voluntary poverty may also be part of such a person's gift mix. This is not necessarily so, however. One of the great

tragedies in the history of the church has been the in-stitutionalising of these two gifts and the uniting of them together. Some full-time workers (including clergy) may have one or both of these gifts. Lay people may also have one or other, or both, of these gifts.

The Bible seems to assume that those who are physically able to marry should normally marry unless they have the gift of celibacy.

What do we say to those who wish to marry but who cannot find a suitable partner? On this specific question the Bible appears to be silent. We can perhaps suggest the following.

1 Corresponding to the special gift of celibacy there is no doubt a general gift of celibacy, in which for certain periods before marriage, during marriage and in widowhood, a person is able to exercise self-control and live a settled fruitful Christian life without intercourse and other benefits of marriage. The single obedient Christian may assume that Christ will sustain him or her throughout life. The single person who wishes to marry should take reasonable steps — especially in terms of develop-ing his or her whole person, spiritually, emotionally and physi-cally — so that he or she is restfully ready to marry should that be God's will.

2 Paul's contribution to the biblical view of sexuality is to em-phasise the great benefits of singleness. As those who wish to marry (and who consider that they do not have a special gift of singleness) wait for and seek a suitable partner, they should give themselves to Christ and his work. The extra responsibil-ities of their later marriage may prevent them from giving the time and effort to the Lord's work which they can now give. We assume that mostly those with this gift are able to live fulfilled and contented lives without marriage. It may, however, be true that some with this gift have a much greater struggle than others. For the dedicated Christian an overwhelming desire to marry may generally indicate an absence of this gift.

We assume that an essential sign of the special gift of celibacy is the ability to live a self-controlled life without marriage (1 Corinthians 7:9). This does not mean that celibate people will not face temptation. They are, however, able to continue to resist this temptation.

The most important thing for each of us to recognise and do is the will of God, whether that be in singleness or in marriage. Let us dedicate our marriages or our gifts of celibacy, together with all our other gifts, to Christ and to the service of his kingdom.

Additional comments

It is important not to stress too strongly the argument concerning the advantages of singleness. As we have seen Scripture appears to teach that for those who are given the gift of celibacy there are certain advantages for the kingdom of God in that singleness. This does not necessarily imply that being a parent and giving attention to children is less the Lord's work or less of service to the kingdom than, say, fuller involvement in the work of the church. Indeed activism in the church may be a way of opting out of handling the intense and trying relationships involved in living in a family. Also, those who are married often have a greater opportunity to serve families than those who are single.

Both married and single people are needed. Whichever state is the Lord's will for you that state will have special opportunities and advantages for service.

Gift 23
Hospitality
1 Peter 4:7-10

Lillie has the gift of hospitality. She loves to open her home to friends. Often members of the church have gathered around the organ in her home and praised the Lord through singing many of the old hymns. Invariably the highlight of this time of fellowship is a beautiful supper which Lillie has delighted to prepare. I dedicate this section to her — and to the many who throughout my ministry have shown to me and my family gracious and generous hospitality.

The general gift of hospitality

In the New Testament the word for hospitality is *philoxenia*, and means literally, love of strangers (from 'philos', loving, and 'zenos', a stranger).

In the Old Testament there is a certain tension in the attitude of Israel to foreigners. Mercy is shown toward the foreigner in the land (Deuteronomy 10:18 f) yet foreigners (Gentiles) are often bitterly opposed. Efforts, however, are made to help foreigners become incorporated into the people of God.

In the New Testament we find the following references to hospitality.

Unconditional love for strangers is taught by Jesus. Strangers are neighbours (Luke 10:29, 36, 37) and one's eternal destiny depends on how we treat the foreigner (Matthew 25:34-35) because the foreigner is essentially Jesus himself. To show hospitality to the stranger is to entertain Jesus (verse 40).

Luke especially emphasises the importance of hospitality (for example 7:36-38, 44-50; 9:51-56; 10:38-42; 14:1). In the parables hospitality is important (as we have seen in Matthew 25). See also Luke 10:34-35; 11:5-6; 14:12-13. Above all, God is depicted as the hospitable Father and the friend of foreigners (for example Luke 14:16 f; 12:37; 13:29; 15:23).

Love implies hospitality (Romans 12:9-13; 1 Peter 4:8-9 and especially Hebrews 13:1-2).

Since in Christ all barriers have been removed Christians are to show hospitality to all — but especially to other Christians (Galatians 6:10; 1 Peter 4:9).

Hospitality should be pursued (Romans 12:13, from *dioko* 'to pursue'). The Greek word here means to chase, as in war or hunting. We are not simply to wait to receive strangers, but to go out and look for them. It should also be done with cheerfulness (1 Peter 4:9) which does not expect reward (Luke 14:12-14).

Hospitality is always a spiritual gift (charisma) whether a general one or a special one (1 Peter 4:9-10) according to the New Testament teaching that all good we do to others is the gift of God (Ephesians 2:10).

Christians must remember that they are strangers and pilgrims on earth (1 Peter 1:1) awaiting the imminent coming of the Lord (1 Peter 4:7-9). They should extend hospitality to companion 'foreigners' as they await the Great Day.

One motive for hospitality is that in exercising this gift 'some have entertained angels unawares' (Hebrews 13:2). This is a reference to Abraham entertaining the three heavenly visitors (Genesis 18) but perhaps also to Genesis 19, Judges 6:11 f, 13:3 f. We do not necessarily need to understand this in a literal sense but in the sense that those whom we entertain may prove to be true messengers of God.[16] Certainly by entertaining other believers, neighbours or foreigners we entertain the Son of God himself (Matthew 25:40).

Hospitality above all promotes the gospel. (See 3 John 8 where the strangers of verse 5 are missionaries in verse 7.) In the earliest days of the Christian era the gospel was taken by wandering messengers who were looked after by the hospitality of other Christians. (Inns throughout the empire were places of ill-repute and Christians did not wish to stay in them.) When Jesus himself sent out his disciples hospitality was to be of crucial importance for the success of their mission (Matthew 10:11 f; Luke 10:5 f). Indeed when hospitality is mentioned in the New Testament the reference is generally to those who are servants of the gospel (for example Acts 10:6; 16:15).

Hospitality was a feature of the establishment of house churches (Romans 16:4 f; Philemon 22; Romans 16:23). Christ is the host. In Christ who is the ideal host, the true meaning of hospitality is exemplified (Matthew 22:2 f; Mark 6:41).

Christ as host is the perfect servant (Luke 22:27; John 13:1 f). He even saves his 'guests' by laying down his life for them (Mark 10:45; Mark 14:22). True hospitality has its origin and goal in Christ who served his guests, died for them and who calls them to the great banquet in the age to come.

The special gift of hospitality

The Bible does not specifically describe hospitality as a special gift (charisma), but it urges all Christians to be hospitable (Matthew 25:35; Romans 12:13; Hebrews 13:2), gives examples of hospitality (Genesis 18:1-8; 2 Kings 4:8-10; John 12:2; Luke 19:5; Acts 16:15) and instructs church leaders to be hospitable (1 Timothy 3:1-2; Titus 1:7-8).

In 1 Peter 4 hospitality is mentioned in the context of speaking about gifts. In the light of the impending end of all things Christians should be sober, prayerful, loving, hospitable and careful in the exercise of gifts (verses 7-10). It may be that Peter speaks of hospitality because it is a practical form of love. The mention of hospitality may have triggered off Peter's emphasis on other gifts as well. Most writers on spiritual gifts agree that this is a serving gift (verse 11). Whereas all Christians, especially church leaders, should exercise hospitality there are those who have a special gift in this area.

Wherever this gift is exercised it is to be done so ungrudgingly. Visitors can be tiring. (An Italian proverb says, 'A guest is like a fish — after three days he stinks'!) Hospitality is to be carried out as to Christ — in a spirit of cheerfulness and generosity.

We may make the following observations about the special gift of hospitality. In its best form it is, or may be as follows.

1 Relaxed. Visitors are received into the home without apology (even when preparations have not been completed or when the house is untidy). Those coming into such a home feel welcome.

2 Exercised without notice. Those with this gift are often (perhaps not always) able to open their home to others without special preparation. Having the gift of hospitality they may generally have a store of food, a bed ready etc.

3 Generous. The special gift of hospitality is accompanied by a generous lifestyle. Visitors are shown a generous spirit.

4 Cheerful. As we have seen, genuine hospitality is characterised by an ungrudging spirit.

5 Exercised with proper priorities. Hospitality which is done for Christ does not suffer from the mistakes which Martha made (Luke 10:40). Hospitality comes before pride. True hospitality is centred on the needs of people. It never imposes itself on people, indulges them or keeps them too long. It is carried out in a spirit of humble service for the glory of God and not as an end in itself.

6 It has a pastoral and evangelistic impact. Like virtually all the other gifts this gift may be instrumental in building up the church in love, faith and knowledge (the pastoral impact) and in making disciples (the evangelistic impact). Those with this gift should prayerfully and strategically plan so that their gift can have maximum impact in both areas.

Questions What are the key characteristics of the biblical teaching on hospitality?

Give examples of how you have benefitted from hospitality?

What are some practical ways of extending the hospitality of the members of your group and of your church?

How can a person with a special gift of hospitality use it for maximum benefit?

Gift 24
Intercession

Recently I was committed to taking a Sunday afternoon seminar and evening service. I had not been feeling well and several factors made me approach this assignment in fear and trembling. I contacted several people in the church who give a good deal of time to intercessory prayer. Jenny is one of them. She senses that this is her special ministry — praying for others.

Sunday's seminar and service were greatly blessed, and although I was very tired even before I commenced, God's Spirit seemed present in considerable power throughout the whole time. I had been upheld by intercessory prayer.

Intercession is not specifically listed in the New Testament as a spiritual gift. However, it is intimately associated with the Spirit in Romans 8:26-27 and although we cannot be dogmatic concerning examples taken prior to Pentecost (and the coming of the age of the Spirit), some biblical characters appear to be especially gifted in the area of prayer, for example Elijah (1 Kings 17:1; 18:1; James 5:17-18. In the latter passage however, his likeness to all believers is stressed rather than the special nature of his prayer.) and Simeon and Anna (Luke 2:25 and especially 26-27, 37b).

Paul is a likely person to have had this gift. The following verses indicate something of the comprehensiveness of Paul's intercessory prayer life. (See Acts 16:25-26, Romans 1: 8-12, Ephesians 1:16-23, Colossians 1:9-12, Philemon 4-6 and the early verses in most of Paul's letters where he often combines prayers of thankfulness with ones of intercession.)

Members of the early church earnestly prayed for one another (Colossians 4:12; Acts 12:5).

Despite the fact that intercession is not specifically mentioned in Scripture as a special gift, people throughout the history of the church have had a special ministry of intercession. C. Peter Wagner identifies Rees Howells, the Welsh coal miner, as one with this gift and describes a church where two intercessors were added to the evangelism team to pray for them as they visited. The number of professions of faith rose dramatically.[17]

Use of the gift of intercession

1 In evangelism and church growth. Outreach ministries need to be supported by those who give a great deal of prime time each week to specific earnest intercessory prayer. It could be that one of the most productive principles of church growth is the recognition of the need for every member of a congregation (but especially those with the gift of intercession) to be interceding regularly for specific persons and families who are outside the church.

2 In revival and church renewal. Research on the history of religious movements shows a close correlation between prayer (especially inter-church corporate prayer) and renewal.[18] Let the members of the Australian church give themselves to private and corporate intercession for the renewal of the church and the awakening of our nation to faith.

3 Support of special ministries. A growing group of Christians support my own ministry. I am conscious of being upheld as I travel and speak in many different places.

Whatever ministry you are involved in it is important that it be supported by the prayers of God's people. Intercessory prayer can be a ministry in itself — a ministry which supports other ministries.

4 Intercession and sickness. In several healing seminars I have discovered that when those who seek healing are supported in prayer in an ongoing way for several weeks they frequently experience a good deal of healing during that period. The gifts of healing and intercession work together. Some Christians may have both these gifts.

Key people in the parish are those who are themselves ill but who exercise a ministry of intercession. Those who through illness or old age are largely confined to their home may have the most strategic ministry of all — especially if they can spend hours every day in intercessory prayer.

The intercession of Christ and of the Spirit

Romans 8 refers to both the intercession of the Spirit (verse 26) and the intercession of Christ (verse 34). Christians have an intercessor within and an intercessor above.

Paul affirms that God is strenuously for the Christian because Christ who died and rose for us is at the right hand of God (the place of authority) interceding for us (verse 34). The metaphor here appears to be the court room. Since Christ is our advocate no accusation against us will be accepted by the divine judge. (See also 1 John 2:1 and Hebrews 7:25)

Romans 8:26 speaks of the Spirit being within us. Here Paul is emphasising the ministry of the Spirit in the weak struggling believer. Paul states that we need the inspiration of the Spirit as much as the mediation of the Son. Sometimes the intensity of our desires moves us to silence. Also we are so burdened by our mortality and sinfulness that we can only groan within. These inward struggles (prayers which are sighed rather than said) should not discourage us. They are the signs of the Spirit's intercession.[19]

We all are very weak. Therefore we must pray. But we do not know how to pray. In our sinfulness and weakness the glorified Christ and ever present Spirit intercede for us. No wonder our prayers are powerful.

Let us all, especially those with a special prayer gift, give ourselves to intercession.

Gift 25
Healing
1 Corinthians 12:9,28

David was ten years old, with a progressively increasing curvature of the spine. He and his mother attended one of our healing seminars and healing service. David almost ran down the aisle to receive the laying on of hands. Since then he has been supported by much prayer. Although his condition has not been cured, his specialist is quite confounded by the fact that the curvature has not progressed to the point where an operation is imperative.

Prof. Donald McGavran has confirmed reports that in many places throughout Asia, Africa and South America where churches are growing, this growth is frequently accompanied by miraculous healing.

I believe that what is needed is a biblical and balanced view of healing which will assist in re-establishing healing into the normal life of the church. This approach to healing will not suffer from excessive claims. It will assist those who are healed, those who are not healed and those who, like David, are partially healed. It will focus on the healing ministry of the whole body of the church and on the special gifts of healing which particular individuals have. Normally, I believe, that this approach to healing will lead to the growth of the church.

Healing in the Bible

1 Creation. God's original creation was good (Genesis 1:10b, 12b, 18b, 25b and especially 31a). Original creation sees God on the side of wholeness and health. Evil (including sickness) is totally foreign to God's original plan as it is to his ultimate plan.

2 Fall. Sin (Genesis 3) results in the fall. All the evil features of fallen creation (including sickness) are the results and signs of this fall (Genesis 3:14-19). While we live in a fallen world we can expect to experience the results of the fall.

In the Old Testament there is a close relationship between sin

111

and sickness and between forgiveness and healing. But as far as the individual is concerned Old Testament Scriptures, like the Book of Job, teach that there is not necessarily a one to one correlation between an individual's sin and his sickness or between his faith and his healing. This is to be accounted for in terms of the strong Old Testament teaching on the corporate (rather than individual) nature of humanity. Sin and sickness are universal and corporate. Although the God of Israel is essentially righteous and therefore punishes and blesses the individual (Jeremiah 31:30) as he or she deserves, the fact of the oneness (solidarity) of Israel (and of humanity) means that sometimes the righteous remain ill and sometimes the wicked prosper.

3 Redemption. God's original creation was good and ensured wholeness and health. The fall marred this creation and resulted in separation and sickness. Redemption undoes the effects of the fall and restores the health and wholeness of the original creation.

Redemption may be represented as follows.

FIRST COMING	NOW	SECOND COMING (Parousia)
Christ died for sins and sicknesses	'Time between the times' healing and sicknesses	Ultimate healing

The above interpretation of redemption provides the basis for a balanced doctrine of healing. Since redemption is in a sense past and complete, the effects of the fall have been dealt with. Christ through his incarnation-death-resurrection-ascension has broken the power of sin, defeated the demonic powers and ushered in the kingdom of God. One of the great benefits of the kingdom is healing.

This, however, is not the whole story. Christians live in the 'time between the times' (between the first and second comings of Christ). On entering the kingdom we enter into the benefits of the kingdom (including healing). But we continue to experience the liabilities of the fall (including sickness).

The kingdom has come with power but it has not come fully and finally. Till Christ comes (i.e. before the parousia) we do not yet enter fully into wholeness. We are not yet finally redeemed.

A balanced teaching of healing recognises that in this life no one is finally whole. It does not offer simplistic solutions to sickness. It ministers to those who are healed and those who are not healed. It recognises that there are many reasons why people are not healed. Lack of faith is only one. It is open to the powers of the kingdom but it recognises both the reality of the fall and especially the need for the return of Christ.

Obviously the church as a body has a large role to play in healing. We, therefore, speak of the healing ministry of the church. This is the ministry of the whole body and in it every Christian shares. When the elders lay their hands on the sick they minister in the name of Christ and as representatives of the whole body.

Any Christian, under the inspiration of the Spirit, may exercise a general gift of healing, but it ought never to be done entirely independently of the body of believers. It should always look to the prayers and fellowship of the body so that it will glorify Christ.

Special gifts of healing

The healing ministry of the church includes the exercise of the special gifts of healing (1 Corinthians 12:9, 28). We note the following.

Gifts is plural. Many commentators feel that this means that there are a whole variety of differing gifts of healing — that some are the channels of healing for certain physical diseases, others are channels for healing of other physical diseases, while others are the instruments of emotional or spiritual healing.

These healing gifts are not given to every Christian. Other Christians have other gifts (verses 8-10).

There is enormous emphasis on both the Spirit and on his sovereignty. Notice how often the Spirit is referred to in these verses. The unity of the body and of the varying gifts is guaranteed by this *one* Spirit. The gifts he gives are therefore spiritual gifts rather than natural talents. The sovereignty of the Spirit in the distribution of the gifts should save the body from envy and jealousy.

It may be that in listing gifts of healing after faith Paul is linking them together. This may suggest that the gift of faith is important in the healing ministry. It may inspire people to receive healing. I also suggest that the gift of prophecy is probably important in the healing ministry. It is possible that the gift of miracles (powers) which follows is also associated with the healing ministry (verses 9 and 29). Powers may, as we shall see, refer to exorcism. Although exorcism is no doubt part of the overall general healing ministry it is always distinguished from the gift of healing. It is a distinct if related charisma.

What I think this material suggests is that there is a general ministry by the whole church and that within this ministry there is a specialist ministry of healing by some Christians who have a variety of special gifts of healing.

Finally we may say that the great need of our day is a balanced ministry of healing-wholeness which is part of the normal ongoing life of the church and which is centred in Christ and in his gospel.

Questions How can your church include within its general healing ministry those who exercise special gifts of healing?

Some of the following could be considered:

a The role of those with special gifts of healing in motivating the whole church to accept its calling in this area.

b The need for those who have special gifts to exercise them within the body rather than in independent meetings.

c The importance of ministers and elders (as representatives of God and congregations in the whole healing ministry) and those with special gifts of healing who may not be elders. Both are important in the healing ministry as are those with other gifts, especially prophecy and perhaps faith.

Gift 26
Miracles
1 Corinthians 12:10,28

In recent centuries in the western church less and less emphasis has been placed on the importance of the miraculous for Christian faith. The industrial revolution, the rise of the technological society, philosophical humanism, secularism, the dominance of science amongst the academic disciplines, the rise of biblical and theological liberalism have all no doubt contributed to a prevailing world view, which permits little if any scope to the miraculous. In recent years, however, there has been something of a reaction against the secularised world-view. Widespread reports from African, Asian and South American churches strongly suggest that in these continents church growth and the occurrence of miracles are related. The charismatic movement is also prompting a re-examination of the miraculous by mainline western churches.

Our task must be to make ourselves open to the fullness of biblical teaching concerning miracles, to keep it in proper balance and to ensure that this balanced teaching is worked out in practice throughout the life of the church (and where appropriate in the community) for the glory of God and the sake of the gospel.

Biblical teaching

Since the kingdom has come and Jesus has opened to us the powers of the age to come we may see the miraculous operation of the Spirit in conversion, answered prayer, healing, exorcism and other miracles.

Since the kingdom has not been consumated — and we suffer the limitations of the fall — we cannot know the fullness of the power of the age to come. Miracles and healings will be limited. Where they occur they may bear the marks not only of the age to come but also of this age. We ought therefore to be open to all the miraculous power which God has for his church in our day as we await the revelation of absolute power in the age to come.

1 Corinthians 12:10, 28 describes the special gift of 'the working of miracles'. This is literally 'the operation of powers' (*energemata dunameon* — hence our English words 'energy' and 'dynamite'). Like the gifts of healing the Greek is plural. (It has been suggested that this indicates that each miracle is a special gift given as the need arises. Or this may indicate a variety of gifts of miracles.)

We really do not know what Paul means here by 'miracles'. He may refer to nature miracles, exorcism or a range of miracles like those mentioned in Acts 13:11, 5:1-10 and the long ending of Mark 16:17-18.

Paul clearly is not referring to miracles of healing for he has just mentioned this as a separate gift (verse 9). Many authorities, including Walter Grundmann, see this gift (really gifts) as acts of power against the invading kingdom of demons, i.e. exorcism.[20]

This interpretation has the advantage of underlining the distinction between healing diseases and casting out demons. These are two distinct gifts and separate ministries.

I favour the view which sees exorcism as the primary reference in 1 Corinthians 12:10. Whether or not exorcism is the primary reference here it seems necessary, at least for the present, to include a separate (if related) gift called miracles to cover a whole range of expressions of power not included under either healing or exorcism. Such powers may include nature miracles as well as those described in Acts 4:30, 13:11, 5:1-10, 1 Corinthians 2:4 and perhaps Mark 16:18a.

We need to bear in mind that Christ himself is the power (*dunamis*) of God and that in his presence other powers are defeated. It is through him alone that miracles are performed.

Conclusion

It is important for us not to over- or under-emphasise the miraculous. Jesus warned that an adulterous generation seeks after signs (Matthew 12:39). We are called upon to live by faith not by sight. We do not depend primarily on what God does but on who he is. Miracles do not of themselves lead to faith. (Recall Moses' miracles before Pharaoh. See also John 6:26-37, 66, 11:44 and 53.) Miracles tend to confirm existing faith rather than create faith.[21]

Widespread reporting of the spectacular can hinder the work of the kingdom (Matthew 8:4, 9:30). Miracles were signs of the presence of the Messiah (Matthew 11:2-5) and of apostolic power (Acts 5:12). Although miracles continue to happen and although there is an ongoing gift (or range of gifts) of miracles we must beware of always assuming that we have the same power as Christ or the apostles.

Priority must be given to preaching the gospel and to the supreme miracle of conversion and character change rather than to other spectacular miracles.

On the other hand we must not underemphasize the miraculous. The view of some scholars that the miraculous gifts were confined to the apostolic age cannot be sustained. This seems not to have been obtained from Scripture but imposed on it. The gifts of miracles were ongoing graces in Scripture and not confined to the apostles. Miraculous gifts continued to be exercised (especially in casting out of demons and in healing) beyond the apostolic age. There appears to be growing evidence that miraculous gifts are increasingly in evidence in our day.

Miracles throughout the Bible glorify God and confirm his word (Acts 13:11-12). Yet miracles are not needed to validate the gospel. Changed lives and the existence of the church do that. Miracles are evidences of God's love and are often given to protect or rescue his children or simply to meet human need (Matthew 14:14-21). It may be that Christians under persecution see this gift more often.

Could it be that a renewed openness by the western church to the authentically miraculous will be a powerful witness to our secular age? For this witness to promote the kingdom of God it must be free from extravagant claims, unbalanced teaching and must not seek to appeal to novelty, fear or excitement. It must also major in the gospel rather than in miracles themselves.

The western church may need to search its heart for signs of the inroads of secular humanism. It may need to replace its world view with a more biblical supernatural one if it is to be open to what the Spirit wishes to accomplish through the church of our day.

Questions Do you think that miraculous gifts are in evidence today?

What factors (if any) could prevent the exercise of these gifts in your church?

Gift 27
Exorcism

A recent crop of T.V. and feature films on demon possession, ghosts, spirits, mediums and Satanism reflects (and probably further promotes) a widespread interest in, and fascination for, the occult. This may be a by-product of, and reaction to, the materialism and secularism of our age. Humans are spiritual beings. We cannot live in a totally non-spiritual environment.

Within the church there is also a reaction against theological liberalism which tended to deny or play down the supernatural (both good and evil) in Scripture and history. There has been a widespread swing within the church back to the acceptance of the biblical teaching on personal evil forces including demon possession. Those members of the western church who have had experience in non-Christian cross-cultural situations have generally found little difficulty in accepting the reality of demon possession. The charismatic movement, despite some extreme emphases, has no doubt played a large role in calling the wider church back to a more biblical stance on both demonology and exorcism.

I believe that it is important for the mainline churches to be open to what the Spirit is saying to the churches in this matter. Let us not retreat from this subject because of the secularism and scientism of our age. Let us take heed of the command of Scripture that we should not let the world squeeze us into its own mould (Romans 12:1). Perhaps more important, let us not retreat from the subject because of the excesses of those who may play on people's emotions (fear or excitement) or who illegitimately make their appeal to novelty.

It is important for all the mainline churches to re-examine Scripture on this subject with openness and readiness to acknowledge the working of God's Spirit in exorcism throughout church history and in contemporary society. It is also important that the church's scholars should contribute to this task so that the church's theology concerning exorcism and demonology is balanced.

Definition

We may say that exorcism is the special facility that some members of the body of Christ have to cast out evil spirits in the name of Christ and by the power of the Holy Spirit. This ability is greatly strengthened by prayer of the church, by discernment and by the oversight of the church's leadership.

Biblical teaching concerning the reality of personal evil forces

In the Greek Old Testament *diabolos* (slanderer, devil) occurs on over twenty occasions. It is always the translation of the Hebrew word 'satan' which means adversary. Whereas it may well be true that there is not a fully developed concept of Satan in the Old Testament the basis for the New Testament doctrine is being established from the first (Genesis 3:1 f).

The only case in the Old Testament which appears to be exorcism is in 1 Samuel 16:14-23. There the Spirit of Yahweh departs from Saul and 'an evil spirit from the Lord tormented him'. We assume here that the Lord permitted this evil spirit to come to Saul.

On this particular occasion the instrument of exorcism was music, and the cure temporary.

In the New Testament both *diabolas* and *Satanas* occur on almost forty occasions. *Beelzeboul* occurs seven times. Other words which are translated 'the enemy', 'the evil one', 'the prince of this world' and 'the adversary' are also present.

Jesus saw his ministry in terms of a battle with, and defeat of, Satan. According to each of the synoptic writers (Mark, Matthew and Luke) Jesus went from his baptism to be tempted by the devil at the outset of his career (Mark 1:9-13; Matthew 3:13-4:11; Luke 3:21-22; 4:1-13). The devil here regarded himself as Lord of this world (Luke 4:6). See also John 12:31; 14:30; 16:11.

In Luke 10 the seventy were sent out by Jesus to announce, 'The kingdom of God has come near' (verse 9). One sign of the presence of the kingdom was that the demons were subject to the name of Jesus when it was used by the disciples. When this was reported to Jesus he responded: 'I saw Satan fall like lightning from heaven' (verse 18). Apparently exorcism was associated with the coming of the kingdom and with the defeat of Satan. Jesus went on to give the seventy authority 'over all the power of the enemy' (verse 19). He nevertheless went on to warn the disciples against rejoicing in this authority over evil spirits. 'Rejoice that your names are written in heaven' (verse 20) he urged. It was more important that they were members of the kingdom than that they had special powers of the kingdom.

The New Testament shows Jesus' ministry and death as a battle against personal evil forces. Although Christ triumphed over these forces in his death and resurrection they remain active. One symptom of the continuing power of Satan is demon possession.

Throughout Jesus' ministry he confronts demonic powers (for example Luke 4:31-37, 40-41; 6:17-18; 7:21; 8:1-2, 26-39; 9:37-43; 11:14-26).

Jesus gave his disciples authority to cast out evil spirits (Luke 9:1, 49-50; 10:17-20) although it is interesting to note that the power is not specifically mentioned in the Great Commission after the resurrection (Matthew 28:18-20; Luke 24:46-49; John 20:19-23; Acts 1:8).[22] The early church, however, did teach about evil powers as well as practise exorcism (1 Corinthians 2:6-8; 10:20-21; Ephesians 6:10-18; Colossians 1:13-16; 2:20 and especially Acts 5:16; 8:6-8; 16:16-18; 19:11-12).

The fact that in the Great Commission following Jesus' resurrection the emphasis is placed on proclaiming the gospel rather than on healing or casting out demons should no doubt encourage us not to overemphasise this ministry. On the other hand the fact that exorcism continued into the new age inaugurated at Pentecost suggests that this is a continuing ministry which the church of our day should not neglect.

It is not correct to say, as some have claimed, that the so called miraculous gifts were confined to the apostolic age. Cyprian (about 250 AD) wrote extensively about exorcism. He taught that an order of exorcists had arisen in the church, that demonic possession resulted in ill-health, that demonic power ceased when a person became a Christian and was baptised, that exorcism could be sudden or gradual and that the primary function of exorcism was to free the sinner in order for him or her to become a Christian.[23]

In summary then, exorcism is not prominent before the coming of Jesus. It is a sign of the coming of the kingdom and Christ's defeat of Satan. It must not be over-emphasized. (See Luke 10:20. The focus in the Great Commission is on the gospel.) Exorcism was a ministry of the early church (both in New Testament days and beyond). There is no need to doubt that it is a genuine ministry for today. The secular bent of our age may have created a special need for it.

Demon possession in New Testament days and beyond was distinguished from other illnesses. We must guard against the tendency towards too readily attributing illnesses to demonic possession. Also cure of disease by exorcism is to be distinguished from cure of diseases by miraculous healing (compare Matthew 9:32-34; Mark 7:31-35). Demonic influence is not necessarily demonic possession. It seems particularly important to warn Christian parents against a too ready tendency to attribute behaviour problems in their children to demon possession. Diseases are usually diagnosed according to their symptoms. Demon possession is the description of a cause. The diagnosis of demon possession should not be the prerogative of an individual but of the body of Christ (especially of the mature leadership).

Demon *re*possession can occur where conversion does not follow exorcism (Matthew 12:44; Luke 11:25). Demon possession may be indicated when the demons are confronted with Jesus (Mark 1:24; 3:11; 5:7). There are grades of demon possession (Matthew 12:45; Luke 11:26). Some demons are more difficult to cast out than others. Intensive prayer is needed before some demons can be cast out. (See Mark 9:29. This verse seems to suggest that the prayer of the church is more powerful than the gift of exorcism. No doubt both should work together.)

The Holy Spirit is of greater power than any other spirit (Matthew 12:25-29).

Jesus had authority directly to cast out demons (Luke 4:36; 11:20). He casts out spirits by the Spirit of God (Matthew 12:28) who elsewhere is called the Spirit of Christ. Jesus' commands are, 'Be silent, and come out of him' (Mark 1:25), 'come out of him and never enter him again' (Mark 9:25), 'Go' (Matthew 8:32). Jesus gave this authority to his disciples to cast out demons in his name (Matthew 7:22; Luke 10:17). On most occasions in the New Testament exorcism takes place in the presence of the demon possessed. Exorcism takes place by a simple command by Jesus or in the name of Jesus. The only exceptions are in Matthew 15:21-28 and Mark 7:24-30 where the Syrophoenician's daughter was healed at a distance without audible command and in Acts 19:12 where aprons and handkerchiefs were carried from Paul to those who were demon possessed. There is no instance in the New Testament of anyone laying hands on or otherwise touching a person who is demon possessed. Modern exorcists usually avoid touch. Exorcism is often accompanied by a final show of defiance (Mark 1:26; 9:26; Acts 19:15). Spirits which are exorcised are like a man passing 'through waterless places seeking rest' and seeking re-entry into the person who has been exorcised (Matthew 12:43).

Controversy surrounds the question as to why Jesus granted the request of demons to enter the pigs (Matthew 8:28). Was there a danger in releasing demons in the presence of people (herdsmen — verse 33)? This may be the reason why modern exorcists remove pets and children before exorcism is attempted.

Exorcism is not necessarily a sign of Christian faith. Jesus said that on the judgement day many will claim entry into the kingdom because of their works, including the works of exorcism, done in the name of Jesus. Jesus will say to those who have not done the will of the Father, 'I never knew you; depart from me you evildoers' (Matthew 7:22-23).[24]

The gift of exorcism is not mentioned specifically in the New Testament as a spiritual gift (unless it is to be identified with or included in the spiritual gift of miracles — 1 Corinthians 12:29) but the many instances in the New Testament, church history and contemporary society convince many scholars that it is a special spiritual gift. The gift of discernment may often accompany that of exorcism. This combination appears to be operating in Acts 16:16-18. It is probable that exorcism should not be employed without this accompanying gift.

Questions See 1 Samuel 16:14. Is it possible that contemporary western society is leaving itself open to the same danger?

Does the cutting of oneself off from the Spirit of God leave one open to other spirits? (Discuss this with reference to the recent interest in the occult.)

What lessons (positive and negative) are there in Luke 10:17-20 for the proper exercise of the gift of exorcism today?

What connection is there between the ministry of Jesus, the coming of the kingdom and exorcism? (See Luke 10:9, 17 and especially Matthew 12:28.)

Is it possible to dismiss Jesus' teaching on personal evil forces as 'views of his time'? If not, why not?

1 Wagner, p. 224.
2 *Theological Dictionary of the New Testament*, Vol I, p. 375 f.
3 Bridge and Phypers, pp. 78-81; Wagner, pp. 96-99. Richard Foster talks about some Christians having a call to voluntary poverty. He does not, however, speak of it as a gift or base it on this verse. (Richard Foster, *Freedom of Simplicity*, Triangle, SPCK, 1981, pp. 116-118)
4 Robert Tuttle Jnr., *John Wesley His Life and Theology*, Zondervan, Grand Rapids, 1978, p. 297.
5 John Telford, *The Life of John Wesley*, New York, Phillips and Hunt, 1887, p. 330. Telford has several pages (330-336) listing Wesley's gifts to the poor.
6 Or was it simply a divine call to him? See *C. T. Studd* by Norman Grubb, Lutterworth, London, 1933, chapter 7, 'He gives away a fortune'.
7 It has been suggested that the disposal of capital was the reason for the Jerusalem Church's later poverty.
8 For a helpful section on tithing see Richard Foster p. 50.
9 Kittel, Vol VI, pp. 700-703.
10 For a discussion of the roles of minister and congregation in leadership see C. Peter Wagner, *Leading Your Church to Growth*, Regal, Glendale, 1984.
11 Wagner, *Your Spiritual Gifts Can Help Your Church Grow*, p. 158.
12 *Dictionary of New Testament Theology*, Vol I, p. 198.
13 See Philippians 1:1. Hermann Bryer thinks that it is certain that deacons and bishops became the bearers of these gifts (Theological Dictionary of the New Testament, Vol III, p. 1036).
14 Robert J. Hillman, *The Church Growing Up and Growing Out*, Unichurch, Sydney, 1981, p. 37 f.
15 R. V. C. Tasker, *St Matthew*, Tyndale, London, 1961, p. 183 f.
16 F. F. Bruce, *The Epistle to the Hebrews*, Marshall, Morgan and Scott, London, 1965, p. 391.
17 Wagner, pp. 74-76.
18 See various works on Religious Awakenings by Edwin J. Orr.
19 On the question of whether or not this is a reference to speaking in tongues, see the debate between Kasemann and Cranfield. See especially C. E. B. Cranfield *The Epistle to the Romans*, International Critical Commentary 1975, Vol I, p. 421 f, and *Dictionary of New Testament Theology*, Vol II, pp. 882 f.
20 *Theological Dictionary of the New Testament*, Vol II, p. 315.
21 Colin Brown, *Miracles and the Critical Mind*, Eerdmans, Grand Rapids, 1984, p. 168.
22 Acts 1:8 is strictly not a commission but a simple promise, 'You shall be my witnesses'. Mark 16:17 which does refer to exorcism is generally recognised as not part of the original ending of Mark although it may reflect a reliable tradition.
23 See Cecil M. Robeck Jnr. *Cyprian, Demons and Exorcism Paraclete* 17:1, Winter, 1983, pp. 18-22.
24 I am indebted to Stafford Wright's article in *Dictionary of New Testament Theology* Vol III, pp. 473-477. 6

6

How to find your gifts

General principles

There is *no* command in the Bible that we should look for our gifts. Why? We really do not know. Perhaps the biblical writers assume that once they have written about the gifts their readers will begin to look for them.

I prefer to think that the biblical writers do not anticipate that we shall have the slightest problem finding our gifts. As we respond to the call of Christ our gifts will emerge.

It may be that a key to discovering and exercising gifts is to be found in the biblical teaching on calling (or vocation). God's call which highlights his initiative and grace, comes to us through Christ and his gospel. It leads to salvation through entry into his kingdom. It results in fellowship, holiness and faith (2 Thessalonians 2:13-14; 1 Thessalonians 2:12; 1 Corinthians 1:9). We note here especially that this call also leads to service (Jeremiah 1:5; Galatians 1:15-16). Paul was called to serve as an apostle (1 Corinthians 1:1).

Ian responded to the call of God to become a Christian and to exercise a vocation of practical service. He exercises his specific helping ministry informally as a technical college teacher, in helping friends and neighbours and by serving as the church property officer. His helping gift draws on a wide range of skills and abilities, including a large mechanical talent.

One aspect, then, of the call of Christ is our calling or vocation. Calling, ministry and gifts seem to be closely related. Perhaps we may say that God calls us to a general calling (vocation). As we respond to the call, a particular ministry in a particular place opens up to us and we are conscious that God provides the gifts that are needed to fulfil our calling and ministry.

I believe that we should be very relaxed about our gifts. Scripture assures each Christian that he or she has at least one gift. We should not be uptight if we cannot describe our gifts exactly.

We may make three general points.

Begin with two categories (speaking and serving) rather than with individual gifts. You may be able to say, 'I think I have some kind of a serving gift', or, 'I think I have a speaking gift'. Then as you become involved in a serving or speaking ministry you will be able to describe your gift in a little more detail, as you find the areas where you are most fruitful and fulfilled. Until it becomes obvious what your precise gift is, a general description will suffice.

You can be exercising your gifts without knowing in precise terms what they are.

The more you know, however, about your gifts the more able you are to use and develop them. Do not be anxious about your gifts, but seek to understand them (and yourself) as well as you can.

Specific principles

1 Centre your life on Christ. The gifts are given by and for Christ. Only as you live close to him can you use your gifts to the full. And as you do this your gifts will emerge and their exact nature will become increasingly clear.

2 Concentrate on the fruit of the Spirit. Gifts can only realise their proper function if they are combined with the fruit of the Spirit which always take precedence over them.

3 Come to the Father in relaxed prayer. (Philippians 4:6)

4 Consider the biblical teaching. Scripture is God's final authority under Christ in all matters of faith and conduct. As you continue to study the scriptural passages which deal with gifts God will show you more about your own gifts. Those who are gifted and trained in the handling of Scripture can help you to apply the Bible to your own life. The prime purpose of this book is to discover the teaching of Scripture concerning spiritual gifts.

5 Consult your God-given aspirations (and feelings) for service. Dedicated prayerful Christians generally find great satisfaction and fulfilment in those ministries which call upon their best gifts. As they respond to God's call they will be drawn towards ministries which use these gifts.

6 Count on the guidance of the Spirit. The sovereign dependable Spirit will show you what you need to know about your calling and gifts and give you any other gifts which are necessary for your ministry in the church.

7 Consider your effectiveness. Normally if you have a teaching gift (plus sufficient training) people will learn when you teach. Evaluate (by faith) the results of your ministry. If your ministry is ineffective it may be that you should be engaged in another ministry where your best gifts could be better used.

8 Consult the body. This is probably the most important principle. It is more important that the church should confirm my call and tell me what my gifts are than that I should inform the church concerning them. (Often we tend to over- or underestimate our gifts.) Of particular importance here is the guidance of the leadership (ministers and elders). Indeed it is one of the functions of their leadership to identify, develop and provide opportunities for the exercise of members' gifts. One way by which the church confirms us in our giftedness is by appointing us to specific offices or ministries in which our gifts will be used.

The special gift of discernment is also important. Those in the body with this gift may be able to assist members in the discovery and exercise of their gifts.

9 Come and be involved. The best (and probably) only way to find one's gifts is to be involved in the ministry of Christ. It is then that the precise nature of your gifts will become increasingly obvious.

10 Commit yourself to experiment and training. It is as we experiment with our gifts that we gain insights into ourselves. It may sometimes be necessary to try ourselves out in certain jobs before we discover whether or not we have certain gifts. Training also is important. Failure in a certain area may indicate lack of giftedness in that area. It may, however, indicate lack of training. Be prepared to give yourself to years of training if necessary in order to fulfil your calling and develop your best gift.

7

Spiritual
gifts and unity

Many Australian Christians (including many within the Uniting Church in Australia) are earnestly seeking the renewal of the church and the awakening of our nation to faith and to the infilling of God's Spirit. What a tragedy if this movement of God's Spirit should be hampered by division and party spirit!

My present ministry takes me into many parishes. It seems obvious that whereas an emphasis on the Holy Spirit and on spiritual gifts is accompanied by new life for many individuals and churches it is frequently accompanied by tragic and hurtful division.

One of the main purposes of this book is to present a balanced biblical approach to spiritual gifts which will not only contribute to the renewal of the church but also to its unity.

We need to see that the New Testament teaching on spiritual gifts is given in the context of unity. The three key passages on spiritual gifts emphasise unity (1 Corinthians 12:12-13, 24b, 25, 28; Romans 12:3, 4, 5, 6-8; Ephesians 4:1, 2, 3, 11, 13). There is something fundamentally wrong if the teaching and exercise of spiritual gifts leads to disunity. Indeed when the ministry of the church is based on a proper biblical understanding of gifts the unity of the church is greatly strengthened. In essence the exercise of spiritual gifts is an essential expression of the unity of the body. It reflects the complementary nature of the various parts of the one body. One person is a hand, another a foot, and so on. All in the body combine together in the one ministry of

Christ under Christ the head as they exercise their varying gifts in love for the building up of the body.

This unity of the body will be strengthened by an understanding of and openness to the biblical teaching on the Spirit of God and on the gifts of the Spirit, especially concerning the following.

1 Pentecost

Pentecost in Scripture is both an historical event and a continuing experience. Many associated with the renewal movement fail to recognise the 'once-for-allness' of Pentecost. The Spirit came as a direct result of Christ's atoning death. Christ's death dealt with all that separated us from the Spirit of God. As a result of Calvary the Spirit could be freely poured forth on a redeemed church. (See John 7:39; 16:7 where the ascension and resulting gift of the Spirit is the final imprimatur on Christ's atonement.) Pentecost, like Christ's death and resurrection, is a unique event in salvation history. It inaugurates the new gospel age — the age of the Spirit.

It is as though in the Old Testament the door into the kingdom was ajar and the Spirit (*ruach*) from time to time blew through the crack. At Pentecost (as a result of the cross-resurrection-ascension) the door into the kingdom was blown off its hinges and the Spirit poured forth upon the whole church! Henceforth the Spirit is freely available (Acts 2:17-18, 21, 38) to all who believe. Pentecost has come. It does not need to be repeated.

Pentecost, however, is also a continuing experience. Although a unique event in salvation history, each person who becomes a Christian must receive the Spirit or be born of the Spirit (John 3:5). The Spirit of the Lord has been poured forth but you and I must walk through that doorway into the kingdom. We must enter into the experience of Pentecost.

2 Baptism and fullness

The phrase baptism 'in' or 'with' the Spirit occurs seven times in Scripture. On six occasions it refers to the contrast between the baptism of John and that of the Messiah (Matthew 3:11; Mark 1:8; Luke 3:16; John 1:26, 33; Acts 1:5; 11:16). This baptism no doubt refers to the whole ministry of Jesus, but especially to the culmination of it at Pentecost.[1] The seventh reference in 1 Corinthians 12:13 teaches that in 'one Spirit we were all baptised into one body'. This includes every believer even the 'babes in Christ' (3:1). It clearly refers to new birth. In becoming Christians we entered into the benefits of Pentecost. On the day of

Pentecost Peter said, 'Repent, and be baptised every one of you in the name of Jesus Christ. . . and you shall receive the gift of the Holy Spirit' (Acts 2:38). This gift is offered to everyone who becomes a Christian. It is appropriate that baptism which is a once for all event should be the sign and seal of this initiating experience of entry into the benefits of Pentecost.

Although it seems best to describe baptism in the Spirit as an initiating event and to identify it with new birth it is important to see that we continue to need to draw on the power of Pentecost. We need to go on being filled with the Spirit. Ephesians 5:18b is present imperative and means 'Go on being filled with the Spirit'. It seems best, then, to speak of one baptism of the Spirit at the outset of the Christian life and many fillings. It is important to note that the initial experience of baptism in the Spirit and the process of filling are both related to the Pentecost event. We need to go on appropriating the benefits of Pentecost.

Much division is caused in the church by denying the reality of the second experience which many Christians claim to have. Wesley observed this two-stage activity of the Spirit and many within the Charismatic tradition testify to it. It is important for the unity of the church that this experience be acknowledged.

In Mark 8:22-26 a blind man needed a second touch in order to be whole. Many Christians (but not all) need a second work of grace. It would be as wrong to make it a requirement of all as it would be to deny its reality in some. The point to note here is that describing this 'second touch' as 'baptism in the Spirit' and insisting that every Christian should have this second experience appears to be inherently divisive because it creates first and second class Christians.

Scripture appears to divide humanity into two groups, although we cannot finally tell who belongs to which group.

Believers	Unbelievers
(wheat etc.)	(tares etc.)

Second blessing theology appears to create a further division by assuming that there are two categories of believers:

Second-blessing	First-blessing	Unbelievers
Christians	Christians	

I suggest that although there are carnal (unspiritual) Christians in the church, there is no clear vertical line between them and other spiritual Christians i.e. there is no absolute distinction between them. Paul described himself as carnal (i.e unspiritual — Romans 7:14, 19). In actual fact a person may be very spiritual

(Christ-like) in some area of life and very carnal (reflecting an unchristlike spirit) in others.

The doctrine of second blessing (as a necessary requirement for every Christian) can easily create division especially if there is a clear sign (like a special experience or like speaking in tongues) to indicate who has 'arrived' and who has not.

We may represent the various views as follows.

Some teach:

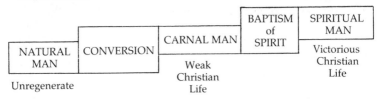

However it appears more biblical to represent it as follows:

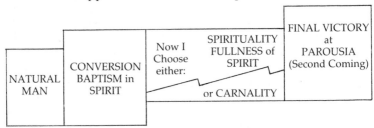

David Watson in his book *You are My God* suggests a third alternative.

Although generally recognised as a Charismatic Watson became convinced of the truth of the second view above. He recognised that in becoming a Christian we are baptised in the Spirit and potentially receive everything in Christ. He points out, however, that the truth that we have in Christ may become ours at various stages. It is like unwrapping a parcel. He says that it is understandable that a Christian who is overwhelmed by the love of Christ and filled with fresh power and joy should describe this experience as 'baptism in the Spirit' although it is not the proper meaning of the Scriptural phrase. He further points out that often those who prefer to speak about 'continuous filling' (rather than a second experience of baptism) do not really expect much to happen.[2]

I believe that the church will be renewed and its unity safeguarded and strengthened as we acknowledge that whereas some (but not all) Christians need a 'second touch' from above we all need diligently and daily to seek to appropriate the fullness of life which we have in Christ and which comes to us continuously from the Pentecost event.

3 Gifts

The whole church should be open to the whole range of gifts (including tongues) which the Spirit wishes to give to the church of our day. To deny this is to exclude charismatics from our fellowship. To do this is to be divisive.

4 Priorities

We need to follow biblical priorities. Division in the life of the church will occur unless the following priorities are observed:

love

faith, hope (plus other fruit of the Spirit)

apostle

prophet

evangelist

pastor-teacher

other spiritual gifts including tongues.

5 Special and general gifts

As we have seen, we need to distinguish between special gifts and general gifts. We need to insist that no one Christian has all the special gifts and that no one special gift (for example tongues) is meant to be possessed by all.

6 Tongues

We perhaps need to acknowledge that whereas not all Christians have a special gift of tongues which they exercise regularly, many of these Christians may exercise the gift of tongues from time to time as a more general gift. Even this general gift does not seem to be given to all Christians.

7 Salvation history

We need to understand the nature of biblical revelation as salvation-history. Sometimes the events in the gospels and in Acts are applied to us today without appreciating that some of the events described belong to salvation history (and are once-for-all events) and some belong to the pre-Pentecost age. Some events (like Pentecost) are in a major respect unrepeatable because they belong to salvation-history. Some experiences (like those of the 120 before Pentecost) or even later events in Acts (for example 19:1-7) are descriptive (describing what happened) rather than prescriptive (describing what ought always to happen).

In order to discover what is prescriptive (and normative) for us we need to refer mainly to the teaching section of Scripture rather than to the historical sections.

8 The age to come

We need to realise that we live in the 'time between the times' i.e. between the first coming and second coming of Christ. Since Christ has come and established his kingdom by his Spirit, spiritual gifts are given to us in abundance. Since Christ has yet to come again to climax his kingdom these gifts are limited and temporary. We, therefore, ought not to over- or under-estimate them.

If the unity of the church is to be preserved we need to be open to the experiences of others. The sovereign free Spirit may give to others experiences which are foreign to us. We must be ready to acknowledge every genuine experience and gift of the Spirit of God.

On the other hand, those who have had special experiences of the Spirit must not be proud of these or insist that all others should have them. To do so is to divide the one body. We need to deal with broken relationships. Christ died to bring reconciliation. The Spirit lives to apply Christ's reconciling work. So no one in his name should divide the body. We should seek to be reconciled to one another, and not let a defensive or proud spirit keep us from dealing with broken relationships.

9 Unity in Christ

In conclusion I refer again to one of the main themes of this book.

To be a Christian is to centre one's life in Jesus Christ as we await his coming. He is God's great gift — his one charisma. All the other gifts which the church has come from that one gift.

We can only possess and exercise our gifts as we are 'in him'. It is only as we are filled with his Spirit that we can use the gifts which he has given us. Only then will the body of Christ be built up until we 'all attain to the unity of the faith and of the knowledge of the Son of God. . . to the measure of the stature of the fulness of Christ. . . to grow up in every way into him who is the head, into Christ, from whom the whole body, joined and knit together by every joint with which it is supplied, when each part is working properly, makes bodily growth and upbuilds itself in love' (Ephesians 4:13-16).

1 Colin Brown claims that according to Mark, Christ's entire life was an expression of the baptism of the Spirit. See *Miracles and the Critical Mind*, Eerdmans, Grand Rapids, 1984, p. 301.
2 David Watson, *You are My God*, Hodder and Stoughton, 1983, pp. 60 f.

8

Bible studies

Study 1 *Ephesians 4:1-16*

1 Verses 4-6 How many times does the word 'one' occur in this passage? Why all the emphasis on unity?

2 Verses 7-8 What are the implications of the fact that the gifts spoken of here are grace-gifts?

3 Since the gifts of verse 8 are given to *each* disciple (verse 7) and not only to the officers mentioned in verse 11, what gifts have you each received? (Describe your gifts if you cannot name them. Assist one another in this task.)

4 Verse 11 If Christ has appointed the officers of your church how should you regard them? (See Hebrews 13:17)

5 Note that all the gifts mentioned in verse 11 are *Ministers of the Word*. (We shall see an emphasis on serving gifts in Romans 12.) What are the implications for your church? Which spiritual gifts are to be valued most highly by the church?

6 Who carries out the work of ministry (verse 12)? What do the special officers mentioned in verse 11 do? What are the implications of this for your church?

Study 2 *Romans 12*

1 Describe in your own words the kind of commitment which is referred to in verses 1-2.

2 What should inspire humility in the gifted Christian?

3 Put into your own words the characteristics of the various gifts listed in verses 6-8.

4 Which are the serving gifts? Contrast the poverty stricken nature of the early church with the affluence of the churches in the west. What are the factors in the modern world which make it imperative for us to exercise our serving gifts?

5 Verses 9-10 Give examples of how some gifts named in verses 6-8 may be perverted unless they are accompanied by love.

Study 3 *1 Corinthians 12*

1 Verses 1-7 In what ways are spiritual gifts contributing to the building up of your church? How can an unbalanced attitude to spiritual gifts create disunity?

2 How is the sovereignty of the Spirit emphasised in verse 11 and verse 18? What practical implications are there in this for you and your church?

3 What are the differences between the idea of the church as a 'bus' and the church as a 'body' (verses 14-26)?

4 What implication does the emphasis on diversity have on the outreach program which emphasises that every member must be an evangelist?

5 How can the work of God in the local church be hindered by a 'hand' trying to be a 'foot'?

6 The individualism of our age may well be responsible for the tendency to consider that specific special gifts (for example leadership, tongues, evangelism) belong to every Christian. Do you agree? If not, why not? If so, how does individualism contradict the New Testament doctrine of the church (verse 27)?

Study 4 *1 Corinthians 13*

1 How does this chapter shed light on the subject of gifts?

2 What steps can your group take to become more loving and to exercise their gifts with love?

3 Verses 8-13 How does a biblical doctrine of the last things (and the coming age) help us to have a balanced understanding of spiritual gifts?

Study 5 *1 Corinthians 14*

1 How does verse 1 justify the church setting aside prime time to study the biblical teaching on spiritual gifts and to assist its members to seek and find the gifts which the sovereign Spirit wishes to give? Why does Paul put prophecy rather than apostleship at the top of the list in verse 1 (12:28)? Why is prophecy superior to tongues? What gifts are most beneficial for the church today?

2 In what ways might tongues speaking in church today hinder worship? Can the use of traditional jargon have the same dangers? Is it possible that with proper order (for example interpretation) tongues could enhance worship?

3 What does Paul's use of tongues tell us about the legitimacy and helpfulness of speaking in tongues, especially in personal devotions? Does it warn us against the denial of tongues as a genuine gift to some? Is it unscriptural to 'squeeze out' of the church those who speak with tongues?

4 In what ways can we today choose the showy and outwardly impressive above that which really builds up the church?

5 What is the outcome of prophecy in contrast to speaking in tongues (verses 24-25)?

6 'Let all things be done for edification' (verse 26b). Worship services were not dull in Corinth! How can proper use of spiritual gifts aid worship? What safeguards are necessary?

Appendix

'Houts Questionnaire' is designed by Richard F. Houts, a Professor of Christian Education at Ontario Bible College, and revised by Prof. C. Peter Wagner. It contains 125 questions and seeks to identify three dominant and three subordinate gifts for each person. It covers 25 of the gifts I have listed. It can be obtained (at the time of writing) from:

The Bob Hillman Foundation,
18 Moore Road,Springwood, NSW, 2777. Australia.